THE TRUTH ABOUT A GIRL
THE STORY OF A FATHER'S LOVE

TRACI WOLFINGTON

Published in Beaverton, Oregon, by Good Book Publishing.
www.goodbookpublishing.com
V1.1

Printed in the United States of America

TABLE OF CONTENTS

FOREWORD

Traci Wolfington has written an incredible book. It took a great deal of bravery and courage to express this level of vulnerability. So this book is not for the faint of heart.

Her story is an intensely personal journey through sexual abuse, forgiveness and a breakthrough of God's love to heal her little girl's heart.

Woven through its pages, a woman emerges despite constant, unthinkable interruptions of injustice and heartbreak. At times it was difficult not to cry out in anger at what Traci lived through over and over again. The effect of abuse is a wild tsunami of darkness in the world today. So many are overwhelmed by their predator's wounds, but *this book is about overcoming*. In this story, this woman's wounds are healed.

I have been Traci's pastor for many years and have watched her deliberately stride into healing, marriage, raising five children and life.

I have seen her set and accomplish a huge goal to become a nurse, while tackling the daily challenges of marriage and motherhood to five children. I have observed her parenting with her husband, Rick, to successfully raise a family that wipes out the stereotypical outcomes of the abused. Rick's strength and love has been a wonderful refuge, providing safety and oxygen for Traci's resurrected dreams. In all this, she has excelled!

Traci has yielded to God and loved Him with all of her heart.

What I particularly liked about Traci's story was the raw, honest depiction of her struggles and abuse. This can help anyone who has been victimized or who knows someone who has been abused. Her story draws you into an intimate view of a shattered heart. For you who have dealt with shame and lies — this book can help you overcome.

I commend Traci for her fearless determination to write her story. If you have been abused, you are not alone. In this story lives the hope of God's overwhelming love that obliterates the effects of sexual abuse. I thank God Traci reached out to Him and for the love and healing He has so freely given.

Dr. Dan C. Hammer
Senior Pastor
Sonrise Christian Center

INTRODUCTION

I can smell the dust from the floor mixed with my tears that are being wrenched from the depths of my misery. A misery so bottomless I don't want to fathom it. It's the floor of the chapel: I cannot seem to pull my face off of it. The pain that is dragging me down to my knees is deep and anchored. The only thought I can seem to formulate is, *This can't all be my grief alone; this is too much for one person.* As I look through my tears, I see to my left and to my right many young people who have joined me on the floor. From stooped shoulders and hanging heads it is blatantly obvious they are hurting, too. In my head I am crying out to God, *You must be showing me their pain? Please let this be their misery I feel! My sobs must be for them? God knows I understand what it is to hurt.*

I was crying harder than I thought was humanly possible, and crying was something I stopped doing a long time ago. When life hurts and disappoints every day, all day, for years on end, you learn to compensate as I had. I turned off the water works years ago and forced myself to put my "I'm okay" mask on. I don't remember exactly when I stopped crying. I know it must have been early on, but at some point I decided I could make it through each day if I refused to acknowledge the pain. I believed tears didn't change anything, they were just a sign of weakness. And weak people can't help themselves.

Now, on the chapel floor, I was beginning to feel that old sense of helplessness again. This was more than the pain coming from the kids kneeling on the floor with me. The panic that was setting in was from a place I knew was not the Lord's: a deep down knowledge that I, like some of these kids, was not okay, no matter how hard I ran from the truth or how hard I tried to deny it. Deep down I knew I could not escape who I was.

In my head I see myself standing at the edge of a cliff. I can't see what is at the bottom of the abyss below me, but I know what's there. The edge is calling me, almost demanding that I step off. I'm either going to jump off into the known places of my past, or I'm going get a hold of myself and force my way back, back to that comfortable stagnant place where I thought I had learned to keep pain and tears in the lockbox that I have made for them. I haven't felt this way, this out of control and this sense of impending doom, for a very long time. It's like playing in the ocean. You see a large wave coming and you frantically run for the shore, but the water is pulling with such force toward the coming wave that you know it is inevitable; you will be overtaken. Sucked back into the deep you are desperately trying to escape.

The cliff is there waiting for my decision. It's pulling at me like the waves in the ocean. I can't stay still any longer; I know what's down in that abyss. It is every horrific memory of the little girl I was. Through the fear that is growing in my head, I hear a faint whisper: "It's your choice."

FRAUD: WILL ALL THE "FAKERS" PLEASE RAISE YOUR HANDS

Just about every year, since the beginning of my marriage, my husband, Rick, and I have attended a summer camp. It is put on by our home church for teens in our area. For the last few years we have held the position of head counselors. Basically, we are supposed to be a support for the camp counselors, deal with discipline issues and help make sure things run smoothly. It quickly became apparent to me at this year's camp that I may be the one needing help to "run smoothly." I was becoming especially familiar with the chapel floor.

The week started in its usual way for me, uncomfortable with my role in leadership. I had always felt camp and church leadership was more my husband's thing, and I was there to support him. He is very outgoing and has natural charisma with kids. We always take our family, and I care for them and help out my husband when I can. This year was supposed to be different. My kids were now old enough to run around by themselves. I wasn't so sure I wanted camp to be different. In my adult life I strive for "the same." I like things in their place, nice and orderly. I had enough chaos as a kid and learned that "different" was more likely to be bad than good.

The thing was, deep down, I knew my relationship with God was not good. I knew I was a fake. But the relationship was steady and comfortable. I knew Jesus had somehow forgiven the "pre-Christian" me, and because of that God would tolerate the current me. I decided this was something I could live with. There had been instances in the past when things would begin to creep into areas I was uncomfortable with. Whether at camp or home, I always had my children to fall back on. I had to tend to them. Besides, some things are best left in the past. At times I felt everything about me was pretend. If people knew the things I had done, if they knew who I really was, they would know I didn't belong here in this role. Yes, some things are definitely best if they are left in the past.

Camp runs from Monday morning, when the kids arrive, to Saturday afternoon, when they load the buses for home, hopefully changed for Jesus and ready to face their new future. The leaders come Sunday night to set up and prepare for the kids' arrival in the morning. We have an evening of prayer to get spiritually ready and then go out for one last tasty meal. Then it's a week of go, go, go, fueled by camp food!

During the week chapel is held twice a day. There is a short time of worship after breakfast with a quick message, and then it's off to play. The night chapel services usually run a lot longer than the morning services. We want to allow the kids time for prayer and to give the Holy Spirit time to do whatever He wants. Our hope is kids, even un-churched kids, come away having experienced God in a tangible way. Hopefully, the teens will meet God in a way they will not be able to deny when they return to their lives. When we are touched by the Holy Spirit, there is always change for the better.

Other than the surprise birthday cake (it was my 35th), Sunday went in its usual way. After the meetings we had an evening meal at Applebee's and a restless night's sleep in an uncomfortable bed.

Monday morning came, and the hustle and bustle began. It was that first Monday evening service when God really started to shake things up for me. I had been struggling for quite some time with my relationship with Him, but as I have already written, I was trying to convince myself that the way things were was best. For a couple of years now it was beginning to get more and more difficult to keep myself from asking the questions I had for God. I knew I had never been loved in a healthy way by a father, and that caused me to question how and if I was loved by a heavenly father, and I was trying to convince myself that it didn't matter to me. It was absolution that I needed, not love and certainly not a "father."

When I looked around at church on Sunday mornings, I could see people adoring God, but I just couldn't find it in myself to feel that way about Him. I knew it wasn't rebellion. It was more a deep sadness. I longed to feel the way others did about God, and I couldn't understand why I didn't. I chose to ignore the issues and pretend everything was fine, rather than risk getting at the truth. I did not want it to be like this, not with the most important relationship in my life.

There was a song we would sing during worship at that time which really spoke to me. One of the verses went, "There has to be more than this." All I could think was, *No kidding?!* These people had something I didn't. I knew I was becoming increasingly jealous. As those words echoed through my thoughts, the jealousy was turning into anger.

I knew God didn't love me the way He loved those around me, but I didn't understand why. I had never understood, and looking back, it was like He had never given me a chance. What I believed He felt about me contradicted what His Word said. I could not help feeling betrayed by Him because of the life I had endured. When I got saved, I sort of viewed my life's story like that of the Bible. There was the "Old Testament" me, where God was harsh and vengeful. And then there was the "New Testament" me, where Jesus had come on the scene and made people acceptable. But why didn't some people ever have to know the harsh, unforgiving God of the Old Testament? Why do they get to see God only through Christ's love and forgiveness? Was it me or was it Him? These questions, along with my past, were best left alone. Why couldn't I just get on with life and be left with the sadness and shame locked away? I really believed, or wanted to believe, that I was okay. I wanted to think that my past had been dealt with because I was strong enough to not allow it in. That's healing, right? It was like having an awful scar on a part of your body you rarely look at because it was easily covered with clothes. My scars were really ugly, but the wounds were closed, and I kept them well covered. As I stated, I was good with Jesus.

Back to "different." I knew that Monday night what I had known for some time: God had been quietly asking me to see Him and know Him differently. But now He was getting louder. He wanted to show me who He was, but only if I was agreeable. I had to be willing to become vulnerable, to not be okay and to not live in my own strength. I had to allow Him to come in and take His rightful place as my Father. That Monday night I was truly frightened. I did not want to give control away, and I absolutely did not want to give it away to a "father."

I remembered crying out to God as a very young child for help, but help never seemed to come. From deep inside I knew there was a God, and I wanted desperately for Him to save me. I now realize at those times when I pleaded with Him to intervene, my little girl heart was asking for a magical intervention. Like a fairy godmother from the movies I loved to watch. Regardless of what I was asking for, I was disappointed in Him. I needed Him desperately, and I felt He had let me down. There were never any fairy godmothers, Daddy Warbucks or magical dragons showing up to save the day for me. I didn't see His hand on me at all when I had needed Him so badly.

As the years passed, I became more and more convinced there was a God, but along with that understanding I became more and more convinced that He must not love me. This was the core issue: I did not love Him because He did not love me.

What father would allow a child he loved to go through the constant hell I had gone through? Only a mean, harsh one could be so callous. I accepted Christ because He had promised to forgive and save me, and I knew I definitely wanted and needed to be saved. But I knew I did not love God because He had not loved me. Not enough, not the way I wanted to be loved.

HIS PROMISE

Before I share what happened between the Lord and I on that dusty chapel floor, I want to tell you about the chaos that was my childhood. The contrast between who I am today and who you might expect from the life I lived is severe. Please understand that God cannot only open blind eyes, mend a broken heart and meet your needs in your finances, He can also heal your heart and change the belief patterns that create your reality. He can heal the wounds that leave gaping holes and nasty scars on your soul.

I believed that being forgiven and saved meant He could now tolerate me. I had no concept of a father's love and only glimpses of a father's healing. His healing didn't mean that I just got to cover my wounds with scars and platitudes, hoping to ignore the shame so I could pretend the scars weren't there. God wanted to make me new. He wanted to remove my wounds, guilt and shame, not just allow me to ignore them with the camouflage of ugly scars. My Father in heaven is that powerful!

When you recognize you need fixing and you allow Him access to those places that are broken in you, He is faithful to restore you. The word *RESTORE* means to "make brand new." The Bible told me I was a new creation. Second Corinthians 5:17 reads, "Therefore if anyone is in Christ, there is a new creation; old things have passed away, and look, new things have come." His

Word also tells me that Jesus was beaten and humiliated so I would not have to be. I do not have to live with the wounds that lead to the scars that became my guilt and shame. God wanted to bring me to a place where I would finally choose to believe His promises and allow Him to finish the work He had started in me.

The Bible promises that He is faithful and just to finish the *GOOD WORK* He started in us (Philippians 1:6). The Lord can heal what is broken in you, regardless of the tragedy of those broken places. I also needed a new understanding of what it means to be healed. God's idea of healing does not include guilt and shame.

I have a very brief impression of the joy of being little. It is there in my memory in quick glimpses, but I have to work hard to recall those brief impressions of carefree joy. By the time I was 4 years old, my young mind knew too much to have the innocent, pure joy you expect to see on a chubby 4-year-old face. My parents had divorced three years earlier, and my mom was a self-proclaimed hippie, enjoying free love and everything that was the early 70s, like enhancing her awareness through the advancements in illegal pharmaceuticals. My father, who is Mexican-American, moved away and wasn't a constant in my life. I think my parents tried some visitations, but I don't remember more than a couple of trips to see him.

Over the next several years my parents would go on to have at least nine marriages between them. My mom married more than five times and my dad at least three. For the most part I think of the men my mother married as numbers on a list. (For the sake of clarity, I will give the ones relevant to my story names, but they aren't their real names partly because I don't remember names clearly and partly to protect their identity.)

In one of the first drafts of this book I had lumped husband number two and husband number three into the same person. Only after confirming some events with my sister did I realize my mistake. I will confess upfront that some of the events I am going to share with you may not be completely accurate, but they are what my little girl mind remembers. When you try and interpret insanity, especially trying to put it in some sort of order, it will never make total sense and will always be at least slightly twisted.

As far back as I can remember, my life moved from chaos to chaos. My mom married her second husband, Deon, shortly after she divorced my dad. When I try to picture Deon, I see him with "mutton chop" sideburns and longish red-brown hair. Very appropriate for the 70s, I guess.

With Deon, my mom, sister and I traveled all over the country. I remember driving for hours at a time and seeing Mount Rushmore and the Redwood forest. I recall climbing onto the foot of a towering lumberjack with his blue ox to have my picture taken. Deon and my mom had converted a long yellow school bus into a makeshift mobile home. At the back of our bus were a few boxes full of keepsakes and mementos my mom had saved. Also in the back were mattresses for sleeping or for my sister and I to play games on when the ride got too long for just sitting. I remember lying on the mattress with her and watching the sky go by, wondering how the puffy white clouds seemed to follow us. Our home was that bus, and everywhere we went all we owned went with us. It was my birthday, so the four of us hopped on the bus to get some ice cream to celebrate. It was the summer of 1974, and I was turning 4 years old. It was a scorching hot day, so my sister and I were very excited about the ice cream.

My sister, who had turned 5 less than a month before, was sitting on the seat next to me at the front of the bus. Since the back had been converted to living space, our house only had the front seats. Shortly after we started out my sister started to complain about her legs being hot, which my mom quickly explained was to be expected since the temperature was more than 90° that day. Deon was instantly irritated with her persistent complaining and warned her to quiet down and stop being difficult. After a few more minutes of her bellowing about her hot legs, my mom finally turned around to see that flames were licking out from beneath the complaining party's seat. Deon whipped the bus over to the side of the road and literally threw my sister and me out onto the soft grass.

Every bit of our lives and history was on that bus. I remember my mom waving her arms and wailing at her husband about all of our baby pictures and possessions being destroyed.

Then, all of a sudden, my mom remembers that not only are our memories burning up on the bus, but her purse was as well, which apparently had some illegal fireworks tucked away in it. She yelled at my sister and me to run as Deon was racing back onto the burning inferno to retrieve the M80s stashed behind the front seat in my mom's purse. Fortunately he was successful in saving the explosives, but unfortunately our home was completely destroyed.

In the chaos of the bus fire the significance of it being my special day was lost. We never made it to get ice cream that day. Looking back, it was almost like a foreshadowing of the rest of my childhood. It started out with so much promise and expectancy of joy, but somehow the significance of my purity and specialness was lost.

My mom thought of herself as a progressive-thinking hippie. So when Deon suggested we start visiting nudist colonies as a family, she was not opposed. I didn't like having to take all my clothes off in front of all those people. I remember being terribly embarrassed to see my mom and her husband naked. The upside in my young mind was that the nudist club we were a part of did lots of fun events, and the camp we visited in the summer was on a lake and that meant swimming. And I loved swimming.

I don't remember where the camp was, but it was a beautiful place to my young eyes. There was a playground with swings and one of those super long teeter-totters that seemed to reach right into the sky. There were wooden tables scattered here and there for picnics and fire pits for roasting marshmallows. The beach area was surrounded by towering evergreens, for privacy, I guess. There was also a clubhouse for indoor activities, but we spent most of our time out under the warm sun playing in the water. While we were at the lake, my mom was very attentive to my sister and me, and I loved that more than anything. Her attention was worth the sacrifice of a little discomfort at being naked, and since I didn't have a choice, I just stuffed to the back of my mind what was out of my control.

Those times spent at the nudist events were the first dents in my armor of purity. We all start out innocent and free of guilt and shame. Psalm 139:13-14 reads, "For it was You who created my inward parts; You knit me together in my mother's womb. I will praise You, because I have been remarkably and wonderfully made." I see now that the lifestyle my mom had us living was a contradiction to what my innocent young mind believed was right and wrong. It caused confusion in my spirit, and the enemy loves confusion. He waits like a cougar ready to pounce at the first sign of weakness in his prey's defense. This was the starting point for the web of lies the enemy would weave throughout the years of my life.

It bothers me when I hear people make the statement, "We are all born sinners." I think it is more accurate to say we are born into a sinful and fallen world and are destined to sin. When we hear, especially as a new believer, that we are born sinners, the perception sometimes becomes "we were born damaged." When a person is already broken and victimized, that statement is easily translated into "I have gotten from life what I asked for or what I deserved." If God knew me before I was born and He truly is my Creator, then I could not have been born more deserving of misery and damage than others. This implies to me that He made a mistake with "my inward parts." Psalm 139:13-14 speaks something different to me; He tells me that I am remarkably and wonderfully made. I wasn't born asking and searching for trouble.

I am not a theologian, and I don't want this to become a theological argument so I will be brief in my explanation. When God created Adam, He (God) created Adam's nature. When Adam sinned, his nature became corrupted, and every human to follow would then also have a corrupted and fallen nature. This is why Jesus Christ had to be born of a virgin and life had to be breathed into her by the Holy Spirit.

Jesus was not born with a corrupted and fallen nature. He lived in perfect relationship with His Father without sinning; this enabled Him to be the perfect sacrifice for our sin/fallen state. Both mainstream Jewish and Christian theology teaches that if an infant or child dies, they will go to heaven. This is because both believe in an age of accountability. It occurs when a child knows the difference between good and evil (or right and wrong choices) and understands there are short- and long-term consequences for both. A child may recognize at 2 or 3 that she will be placed in timeout or spanked for doing something she is not supposed to, but she may not understand the long-term lesson and consequences of her choice.

Jesus tells His disciples not to turn away children and, in fact, tells them they must become like children (Luke 18:17). I believe our being born with a corrupted nature (I use the term corrupted nature instead of sinful nature, as so many Christians do, because God made and gave "man" his nature. God did not and cannot create sinful things.) is much like other laws of nature. The Law of Gravity tells me that if I step off the railing of a 100-foot bridge, I will fall; it is inevitable, and it will happen. Being born with a fallen nature and having free will, I will sin. Once I have the knowledge and understand the difference between right and wrong, I will sin, and I will make sinful choices. But there is innocence in children that the enemy slowly whittles away. We try to protect our children for as long as possible, hopefully until they are mature enough to exercise self-control and stand for righteousness. Whether you agree with this explanation of our children's innocence or not, I hope that you will bear with and hear my message.

The time I spent naked in front of so many people was the beginning of a belief system the enemy was creating for me about myself. He was wearing down boundaries I would naturally have about my body, mind and spirit. The devil is a predator, and he starts on us young. He wants us damaged and confused so he can penetrate deeply with his lies and deceit.

I want to clarify before I go on: Throughout my story, I do use titles like "the enemy" or "the devil," but I am using these as a generalization. When I use these terms, I am not actually referring to the fallen angel, Lucifer. I am meaning his purposes in general. I am not in any way saying that I think the devil himself messed with me personally. The Bible tells us that one-third of the angels fell with Lucifer. They have been around for a long time, learning just how we work. I am not implying the devil is omnipresent. Ephesians 6:12 reads, "For our struggle is not against flesh and blood, but against the rulers, the authorities, against the powers of this dark world and against the spiritual forces of evil in the heavenly realms." It is the spiritual forces of evil I am referring to when I say "the enemy."

I had a clear revelation that week at summer camp as to just how deep the enemy can penetrate your soul, even when you believe you have a pretty descent handle on things. Before that time I spent with the Lord on the damp chapel floor, I didn't understand just how much damage my past had currently inflicted on me. I had an understanding of how bad it was. I could see it on people's faces when I shared parts of my testimony. But I didn't grasp the extent of the wounds that were lying closed and ugly far beneath the surface of who I had become. God was showing me that I was wearing all my unshed tears as a badge of accomplishment. He was showing me that He wanted every part of me, including my shame and tears.

The Lord wanted a "new creation." I now see the significance of the words "born again" when I think of the new creation we are in Christ. When my children were newborns, their skin was smooth, flawless perfection. Life had not put any blemishes on them. In time they would fall off their bike and skin a knee, trip over some unseen object and need stitches or befall some other injury; but as newborns not one had a single scar. The Lord wanted me "born again," like my newborn babies. That meant no ugly covered wounds, no scars, no guilt and no shame.

FROM CHAOS TO CHAOS

If there was one constant in my life as a kid, it was inconsistency. The one thing I could always count on was change. My mom was forever moving on to something or someone else. Husband number two didn't last long after the bus incident. He had a mean streak with a short fuse, and he would hurt my mom sometimes. There was often a lot of yelling and swearing between them. My mom moved on from Deon, and we went to stay with her dad, my grandpa, for a while. My grandpa was a gruff old guy, but he was basically good to us. I remember my sister and I didn't want to cross him because when we were naughty, he would give us a thump on the head with the stump that used to be his index finger. He had lost the top half of the finger in some sort of accident, and since he was more than twice my height, the tip of that stumpy finger reached the top of my head handily.

It didn't take my mom long to find herself husband number three, Doug. I think I was just about 5 years old. I recall being excited at first because my biological dad had not been around much for as long as I could remember, and this new man wanted my sister and me to call him daddy. I liked him. At first he made my mom laugh often, and when she was happy, she would be silly with my sister and me.

Not long after my mom married Doug we moved from my grandpa's house into Doug's parents' place. Then my mom and Doug left. My mom told my sister and me they were going to go and try to get things set up so we could have a place to live. I don't remember how long we were at his parents' house without them, but it always seemed like a long stretch of time when I wasn't with my mom. I don't recall really minding being left with these strangers that were now my new set of grandparents. They were friendly, and my sister and I often got to tag along on camping and hunting trips with them and their vast family. Family seemed to be important to them because there were always relations stopping by. It was a busy, cluttered house most of the time, but it was a "home," and I liked that.

These new grandparents were kind of roly-poly but at the same time no nonsense. My sister and I needed care, so they took care of us. It sticks out in my memory that they loved to eat, and certain foods had to come from certain places; grocery shopping was a serious event that took all day and involved driving long distances to get the best deals, and I was not allowed to come. Doug's mom would make homemade coleslaw; it seemed we had it with every meal. I probably just remember it that way because I didn't much care for coleslaw and a heaping helping seemed always to be on my plate at any afternoon or evening meal. She also showed us a new way to eat our morning eggs. She would fry them "sunny side up," then turn them out onto a plate to be mutilated into a hot, gooey mess. This is still my favorite way to eat them, as long as all the white is cooked!

When I look back and try to think of what it was like

with them, I see my sister and me as strays they were willing to take in because they were decent people. Sort of like they were humane and weren't going to turn us away, but they didn't have any real attachment to us. Like feeding the neighbor's cat or dog because you feel sorry and obligated.

Doug had a younger sister and two or three brothers. His sister was young enough to be in high school, so she still lived at home. One brother who was also at home was not much older than her, and he spent his time working on cars and racing them at the speedway. When I think of him I can hear the roar of late nights at the races watching him try to win the privilege of kissing the pretty girls who brought out the trophies. That was another thing I liked about staying with my new family: They were so into racing cars. Their front and backyard was like a graveyard of old cars in various stages of disrepair. The different men who came and went were always pulling one part out of one corpse to use in another slightly more living car. My sister and I were free to play on and in them, as long as we were mindful not to get hurt.

Other than the younger brother still at home, only one of Doug's other brothers stands out in my memory. This brother was quite a bit older, and he didn't live at the house with the rest of us. I remember he also shared in the family hobby of working on cars. He had his hands under the hood of cars so much so that the creases of his fingers were permanently stained and grimy; grease was always caked under his fingernails. Every finger was nasty with the remnants of car grease — all except the middle finger on his left hand. That finger was always perfectly clean because it rarely left his mouth. He was always sucking on it the way a 2 year old might suck his or her thumb. I remember thinking that his mom should not let him do that anymore. Even at 5, I found it creepy. He was always sucking on that finger, while the rest of his nasty hand hung from his filthy face.

This particular brother came to visit often. His name was Chet. I started out really liking Chet. He was fun and always extremely attentive to my sister and me. He was quick to play tickle games and give hugs. On one of his visits, he took my sister and I out to the trailer parked in the front yard to play house. The trailer was one of those ancient bubble-shaped ones. It reminded me of a big fat beetle bug. I had wanted to play in it since the first day I had come to stay with this new family, so this was really a treat. I was so excited to be allowed in the trailer and even more so because Chet desired badly to play with us.

That was the first time I clearly remember being molested. At first he didn't really hurt me physically, and I don't remember exactly not liking the game. The abuse by Chet went on over the next few years, and I grew to hate the game more and more. I was in desperate need of love and attention, as is every child, but especially as a child of divorce who didn't have a father, didn't have a home, didn't have a mom that was a constant, stable protector and really didn't have a consistent adult in her life to love. As I grew older and the abuse escalated, I hated myself for wanting to keep the secret. I can't say that in the beginning I knew what was happening was wrong. After all, wasn't this love and attention? But inside I always knew I didn't like the way it had to be.

At 5 years old, a child wants and needs to be loved, and a child will be faithful to that love. Much like a dog that is continually beat but still loves its master because it is the only love the dog knows. It would be like saying the dog loved to be beat, therefore, the dog not only deserved it but asked for the beatings by its loving master. In reality, the dog can't help it; it was created to be relational, a pack animal.

GLASS FLOORS

It is the first day of teen camp, and I am overwhelmed with mountain-sized emotions. I am a blubbering mess, sinking deeper into the carpet with every desperate worship song booming out from the worship team. And worst of all, people are starting to notice. I had come to camp intent on being there for all those kids, but now I'm gripped with sobs that I can't seem to hold in and a fear I can't seem to shake. I was asking God to please use me this week. The harder I tried to keep the tears from coming out of my eyes, the more they were escaping from the other holes in my head. Define blubbering: secretions coming from eyes, nose and mouth simultaneously.

My younger children were at camp with us, as they always were. Kenidy was 12, Ryleigh 11, Trinity 8 and Jaden 6. My oldest daughter, Tiffany, was 20 and already living on her own. Trinity and Jaden were off playing in the foyer, but my two older girls were witnessing what was happening to me, and they were becoming very concerned. Their mother did not fall apart like this, and they did not understand.

Once worship ended and the guest speaker, Daren Lindley, was making his way up to share the message for the night, I began to pull myself together, somewhat. I took a seat at the back of the chapel so I would be available to my younger children if they needed me.

Pastor Daren was speaking about a man who had been tragically abused by his father and the contrast to who he was today, due to the grace of God. As he was relating the story, I felt myself starting to become sick inside. Not exactly physically, but somewhere deep inside I felt ill. I knew I couldn't sit and listen anymore. I had to get out of there, or things were going to get very uncomfortable. I could feel the anxiety creeping back and the tears beginning to well. Over the years I have heard many tragedies and triumphs. So why was it bothering me so much now? Why the emotions and the fear? Why was the anger seeping in?

I wanted to yell at somebody and use my fists to make them understand how unfair life was. I wanted answers. I was so hurt and so angry at that moment, listening to another story of pain that wasn't right, pain that was not deserved. I needed to understand this God who was supposed to love us.

After sitting through the end of that particular message, my husband and I went back to our room. I told him a little about what was happening to me. I told him how overwhelmed I was. I told him I must be feeling the despair these kids are feeling. The disappointments and hurts they had endured. I told him my feelings were so huge and my fears so real, I didn't think I could live through a whole week of this pain. I told him I thought some of the campers must be living through what I did because the pain felt so familiar.

My husband asked me if I wanted to speak with the

pastor, but I told him I didn't need to. He told me he was concerned because, as I wrote above, people were noticing (including him) that I was not myself. In our 14 years together, he had only seen me cry two or three times. But, after all, this week wasn't about me, it was about the youth that were there to encounter God. And this was a great excuse to ignore my issues.

So I tried to stuff down what was happening in me and focus on being available for the teens. Besides, I still had my doubts; how could I speak to these kids and convince them God loved them and everything would be okay? I had my own doubts as to which God they may encounter. Would they experience the loving New Testament God, as some people did? Or would they be like me, forever having to convince themselves that they were okay because at least Jesus could forgive them and help them forget …

I managed to stuff things down by hiding in my room or burying my nose in my Bible and looking very unapproachable. Everything I did was to hide the fact that I was walking on glass and could crash through at any moment. I felt weak, and I didn't like it. It had been a long time since I had felt so weak and out of control. I did not want to remember what that was like. I had been the one asking for more from Him, for something deeper, but now I wasn't so sure. He wanted to take me back so He could bring me forward.

෯෯෯

After that first initiation into our new secret relationship out in the trailer, Chet would often give me reminders of what had happened. He liked to sit me on his lap so I could feel his privates on my backside or discreetly fondle me, regardless of who else might be around. Sometimes it was just a wink or a squeeze that was meant to remind me I was for his pleasure. He would whisper in my ear that I had made him hard or call me a vile sexual pet name in front of anyone to remind me of our "special" secret relationship. It was like he wanted me to know that everyone knew, it was okay and there was nothing I could do about it. But at the same time, it had to be a secret. This was terribly confusing for me. Was it wrong? Was he embarrassed because of me? Did no one, or no being, care to help me? Was this what love and affection was?

At some point during the years that he was abusing me, Chet decided to rent a room in our house. He was often the babysitter to my sister and me when my mom and Doug would go out at night. On those nights we would all play "house."

A single mom and her two sons were our next-door neighbors at that time. Averie, the mom, was a tiny little elfish woman with a squeaky small voice. I remember we would joke about how funny it was that she was only slightly taller than my sister and me. Her two sons were 14 and 18. The 14 year old, Drake, was tall for his age, with a stocky build, which I thought was strange coming from such a small woman. He had dark hair that his mom kept short in a buzz-cut, and I remember thinking his eyes were too far apart on his face. The older brother, Lloyd, was even taller than Drake with long, greasy dark hair. He always seemed to wear dark clothes, and I rarely remember seeing him smile. Where Drake was pretty outgoing, Lloyd was a quiet loner type.

Our families were together often having barbeques or just hanging out. I remember liking Averie's funny personality. My mom and Averie became close friends quickly. The boys didn't hang out with us too much because of the age difference, but they were always nice enough to my sister and me in front of the parents.

But it wasn't long before Chet and the boys realized they had something in common. Chet invited them over one night when he was babysitting my sister and me, and the neighbor boys joined in the "game." Most times only the younger boy would come over, but sometimes both would join in.

For the most part the games were not too violent. Chet used manipulation more than force to get me to agree to things I didn't want to do. He would try and make it seem like I had a choice by asking things like, "Do you want to be with me or him?" I learned to be passive and non-confrontational so it would just be done and over.

On the nights when my mom and Doug were home, Chet would come and visit either my sister or me in the room we shared. It didn't matter to him that my mom and Doug were in the room right next door. He was very bold and obsessed with us. He would wake me up and remind me to be very quiet so we wouldn't get caught. So many nights I woke to him on top of me whispering and touching. I remember hoping that my mom would walk in and accidentally find out so it would stop. On the other hand, I didn't want anyone to ever know the humiliation I was living in. As I recall that time in my life, I can almost feel the exhaustion. I was so tired all the time, and I remember just wanting to sleep. I dreaded nighttime because I knew he would be there to interrupt my dreams. These were the first times I began to cry out for God to please save me. He didn't.

One of the things I hate about sexual sin against an innocent is that it wraps guilt and shame so tightly and securely around your soul, you begin to live with it like it actually is a part of who you are. Eventually it becomes so engrained that it *does* become who you are. Even the "healed" in our society are referred to as "survivors."

I hated that term because to me it still equaled "victim," or more accurately, victimized. I believed down deep that people said nice things about me when they heard my story because they were embarrassed for me. I could never tell them all that had actually occurred, all that I had actually agreed to, or they would know how shameful I really was.

Through our shame, the enemy weaves a web of lies that becomes our reality. His deception caused me to believe that perversion was love. Not only that, but I also believed I liked and desired that kind of love. Therefore, I was shameful. Because of the lies, which had become truth for me, the natural conclusion I reached was what a pervert I must be. I was undeserving of good things.

For many years afterward, I would be told again and again by the different therapists in my life, "It's not your fault. Repeat after me, it's not your fault." I heard and quoted that phrase so many times, I actually began to believe it with my head. But until the truth spoke to my heart, they were just empty words.

What I had wanted was to be loved. I was missing my mom, and I was missing a connection with these people I had been left with. Because of the circumstances I was in at that time in my life, I was an easy target for predators. The biggest lie ever told to me by the enemy was "you wanted this" or "you deserve this." It isn't a lie he came up with especially for me. Before me, many childhood victims of molestation have believed it is their fault, and many will tragically believe these lies after me.

My reality was made of lies from the pit of hell. In God's reality, I just wanted what every little girl desires: to be loved and cared for, to feel secure, to be free to be little. I hope you are beginning to see the truth of scripture when it reads, "All sin leads to death" (Romans 6:16). The sins that are committed by us or against us lead to a physical, mental and spiritual death.

My first big "ah-ha" moment came when I was around 14 years old. I had an epiphany. I realized I didn't consciously or unconsciously ask for that kind of attention from men. I was not some overtly sexual 5 year old. I began to realize and believe in my heart that what happened was not my fault, and I knew I did not want to be victimized anymore. It was not the repeating of the words told to me by my therapists. It was the beginning of my heart opening to my Creator. I began to realize in some strange way that I did not know or understand love but desperately wanted to.

God created us for relationship. Relationship is something we desire from the moment we are born and put into our mother's waiting arms. Because I wasn't receiving the affection and consistency my young heart was made for, I was an easy target for deception and abuse. It's strange to me that I don't remember where I was or what was happening to me at the time of that marvelous revelation, but I distinctly remember the impact of it. Just this small exposure to one of the giant truths God had for me was like this enormous relief washing over me.

Matt Damon portrayed an "ah-ha" moment perfectly in the movie *Good Will Hunting*. Robin Williams plays a physics professor at the university where Damon's character works as a janitor. Damon's character, Will, is a mathematical genius but is so broken by his past he refuses to risk finding out what he might accomplish with his gift. There is a point in the movie where Williams' character gets at what is haunting Will. He tells Will that his past wasn't his fault; it wasn't Will's fault that his father beat the crud out of him as a little kid. He hadn't asked for the hateful abuse that was inflicted on him.

All of a sudden, after kind of laughing it off and saying

"I know, I know," Damon's character gets it. He completely loses it as the truth of those simple words takes root in his heart. "It wasn't your fault."

When the truth hit my heart like a sledgehammer, I was furious, sad and relieved all at the same time. I was furious at the deception, sad because of the memories that caused me to believe that deception and relieved to finally know the truth. The difference between being held and loved and being groped and abused by a tormenting pedophile was impossible for my young mind to see clearly before. It had been easy for me to believe I had gotten what I had desired and deserved. I was looking at myself through a carnival mirror. I was seeing the twisted version of God's beautiful creation ...

Truth is absolute and never changing; truth is God's reality. The truth is that Chet and the others were manipulative, sick and totally controlled by the enemy. The reality was and is that I was an innocent child starved for affection and attention. I was a perfect target for the enemy.

Remember: He hates us all from the moment we are conceived. The enemy's only purpose in this world is to destroy as many of us as he can. He has no mercy. God's Word reads in John 10:10, "A thief comes only to steal, kill and to destroy. I have come that they may have life and have it in abundance." To finally realize the abuse foisted upon me was not my fault was a major revelation for me. It allowed me to get out of the "victim" cycle, meaning I knew what happened wasn't my doing, wasn't okay and would not happen again. But I still did not know what love was, what a healthy relationship was and, worst of all, I had no idea how to deal with the shame and guilt that had become my constant companion.

༽ེ༽ེ༽ེ

Recently I accompanied a good friend of mine to a Bible study she was teaching to a group of women. In her teaching, she described shame as ashes that follow us around. I thought this was an excellent picture of shame. When she said it, I saw in my mind the ashes of shame circling us, like our own personal tornado that only we can perceive. Occasionally the ashes die down a bit and settle at our feet, but as soon as we begin to move forward, the ashes are kicked up into their whirling, consuming pattern again. It is like a dark prison of shadows always surrounding us, gripping us and often choking the joy out of us.

Shame keeps us repeating the same patterns, making the same choices, leading to the same outcomes. Around and around we go. Our prison becomes our safe haven of what is comfortable and familiar. We grow to hate the feelings and the chaos of our emotions and poor choices that have come to define our lives, but we can't seem to escape the cycle that shame keeps us in. Lies become truth.

Throughout my walk with the Lord, He has shown me that I must be willing to take action in order to walk into what He has for me.

GLASS FLOORS

When I was 14, He revealed to my heart that it wasn't my fault, but it would be many years later that I would finally be willing to give up the ashes of my shame to lay at His feet.

FEAR

It is the second evening of teen camp. The daytime has been easier for me. The daytime has always been easier. As a child and through my teen years, I suffered terribly from anxiety attacks and night terrors; I had only spent two nights here, and already I was so tired of dreading the night. As everyone is filing in for chapel time, I am filled with part dread and part excited anticipation. The music begins, and the weight of the Holy Spirit is dragging me to the chapel floor once again. God's presence is on me in a mighty way, and I am, again, a weeping, pitiful mess. The despair mixed with something else I can't name was becoming suffocating. I begin to question God, while mopping the floor with my soggy eyelashes. "What is going on? I don't know if I want to feel this. Why are You humiliating me like this?" I was hurting, I was embarrassed and now I was angry.

I did not want to be so vulnerable in front of so many people. I knew I was receiving what I had been asking for from the Lord. I desperately needed more intimacy and understanding. Most of all, I wanted to know and love Him in the way I saw so many others around me doing. But couldn't I do it on my terms? I did not know if I could risk loving with abandon, with innocence. What if He let me down again? What if I really believed, like that child I used to be, and He did not answer as He had not then?

Psalm 40:1-3 speaks a truth that I desperately wanted to understand and believe. "I waited patiently for the Lord; and He inclined to me, and heard my cry. He also brought me up out of a horrible pit, out of the miry clay, and set my feet upon a rock, and established my steps." As a little girl, I felt deserted by God and everyone else. That belief stuck with me into adulthood. Up to this moment, it had followed me all the way to the smelly chapel floor.

I didn't even try to make it through another service listening to stories of pain and triumph. I didn't feel so triumphant anymore. So instead I hid outside the side door to the chapel. My husband asked me later if I was "okay." I had been just "okay" for so long. I was embarrassed to tell him I wanted so much more than "okay." I had always been so proud of my okay-ness because it was really so much more than you would expect from my circumstances, from where a person like me had come from. I was a survivor, wasn't I? I was beginning to question what that even meant to me.

When I was around 7 or 8, my sister told my mom what Chet was doing to us. I don't remember exactly how my sister came to tell on him. I can see the vacuum cleaner running and my sister crying on the couch. My mom had to turn it off to hear what she was saying. Chet had moved out, and I think my sister felt like this might be our only chance to tell before he came back. I was on the couch, also, quietly watching. I remember feeling detached, as though what was going on between my sister and my mom was far away. When my mom turned to me and asked if what my sister was saying was true, I could only nod my head yes.

My sister and I never saw Chet again. At some point the neighbor boys and their quirky little mother moved away, also. I don't even remember if my sister told about their part in the "games."

My mom informed the authorities, and we were taken to a doctor for a physical. I didn't really mind telling the woman doctor what Chet had done to me. There was numbness in me now that sheltered my mind from the truth of what had gone on. I was just relieved it was done and he was gone. Unfortunately, just because he was gone didn't mean the scary things were over. Doug was still there.

Fear. I hate the weakness of fear. It brought me right back to being a little girl and having no control over anything, like a marionette with its strings in someone else's hands. I was right back to being at the mercy of someone who seemed to take pleasure in making me afraid.

I saw my mom's third husband, Doug, as being a scary man. Not at first, of course; at first he was charismatic and fun. But over time he showed himself to be mean and brooding.

From what my mom has told me, he was into a variety of illegal things. She was never very specific about what those things were. Throughout their marriage, aside from the time my sister and I lived at his parents, we seemed to be on the move a lot, from one place to another. I don't think we ever stayed in one place for more than a few months at a time.

There was a period after they were first married that Doug took us to live up on what I recall was a deserted mountaintop. It was after Chet's initiation in the bubble trailer but before we lived in a house with Chet in Edmonds. We lived in two small travel trailers situated in the shape of an L on a spot cleared of trees. My sister and I slept in one trailer, while my mom and Doug slept in the other larger one.

I didn't like it up there at all. It wasn't fun like the camping trips I had been on before with Doug's parents. In my little girl world, ghosts, goblins and hairy monsters were very real, and I was certain they lived up on the mountain at the fringes of our makeshift homestead. Not long after we settled in, we found our kitten drowned in a mud puddle and our dog stabbed to death. I knew that whatever killed our pets must have been terribly strong and evil because our dog had been a massive brute. I think he was actually part wolf.

It isn't clear in my memory if my mom actually told my sister and me somebody didn't want us on the mountain with them or if I overheard her and Doug talking about it. I pictured 7-foot-tall Sasquatch men with clubs and axes laying claim to the mountaintop we were currently inhabiting. I was relieved that not long after the dog incident, we obliged the mountain monsters and left the lonely mountain and the dream of making a life there.

At some point after staying with the grandparents and

living on the mountain, we moved to a farm in a rural area of Western Washington. We had various animals to care for, including a calf and a pony named Peanut. It seemed like Doug always had some new plan for our lives. I remember being so excited about getting to go out and feed the gangly calf with a baby bottle. We also had cute little piglets that were born when it was too cold for them to stay outside, so they got to live in the house with us for a short time. It was all very exciting for me. I loved all of the animals so much so that I didn't even mind the smell that seemed to cling to every piece of clothing I put on.

One day Doug wanted to teach my sister and me something important about being a farmer. He took us out to the barn where the hefty daddy pig lived. Doug felt it was important for us to watch the slaughtering of the hog so we had a clearer understanding of what it was to be a farmer and where food really came from. I watched as he slit the animal's throat and let it bleed out until the massive pig finally stopped flailing and squirming like a fish on the end of a hook. I didn't much care for that particular hog, but I didn't think it deserved to die such a gruesome death.

As the animal hung there in front of us, we had to each take a turn walking up and touching the lifeless carcass. On a different day, Doug showed us how funny it was to chop off a chicken's head and watch it run in frantic circles searching for where its head might have landed. Normally I would have agreed that these particular practices are just the realities of farming, but even at 6 years old, it seemed like Doug took a certain pleasure in watching us witness the bloody deaths of the animals we had made friends with. All of these things played into the fear and terror that gripped me.

At some point the farm failed, and we moved on to the house in Edmonds. As I said before, Chet made occasional appearances on the scene throughout our moving around, so there was not only the fear of Doug and his life lessons but also the dread of Chet's next visit.

I remember another incident when we were all — including Chet — in the house in Edmonds. It was Halloween. We had a little baby goat we kept as a pet, and on that particular night, the goat got out of its pen in our yard and ran away.

Doug, his brother and some of his friends went hunting for our pet. They found the goat half dead after being mauled by some dogs. At least that was the story Doug gave us when he returned. The animal had much of his skin torn from his body in large ragged chunks. He brought us to the garage to see what was left of our pet.

He had rigged up some sort of a sling out of a sheet. The four corners were attached to the ceiling with ropes, and leg holes had been cut out of the sheet to keep the animal in a standing position. Its blood seeping through the sheet, and he was making this awful mewing sound. It was a grizzly sight. Thankfully the goat didn't live long, due to the extent of his wounds. I felt as though the whole thing was a warning: Evil things happen all the time, so be very careful.

I know my mom was very afraid of Doug. He had all the control. I could tell at times my mom was uncomfortable with the things he wanted to do, but she always ended up doing them, anyway. Like the time Doug brought home a huge old-fashioned beer keg and had my sister and I strip down to our panties. He made us drape ourselves on it and over it in many different positions while he took pictures. My mom was there. Everyone was laughing, and it was supposed to be fun. I never saw the pictures; it used to make me feel sick that they might be out there somewhere. I don't know whatever became of them, but I always assumed nothing good.

The only thing I really liked about living in that house in Edmonds was the neighborhood school. My teacher was a pretty dark-haired woman who always seemed to be smiling at me. She often allowed me to stay in with her at recess and help with little jobs. She hugged me often and told me I was special. I was always very excited and happy to spend time with her. When I remember her, it makes me think of sunshine. Maybe supernaturally sunshine was shining down on her, regardless of the weather outside. I know she wasn't really backlit with sunrays, but I probably have that picture of her because she warmed me in places that always seemed cold.

❧❧❧

There is a false reality that the enemy wants us trapped in. Then there is God's reality. God's reality can be found in the truth of His Word. There is a way to be well and whole and everything your Father in heaven created you to be. Psalm 40:11 reads, "Lord, do not withhold Your compassion from me. Your constant love and truth will always guard me."

The first half of this scripture describes what I felt and basically where I stopped and got stuck. But the second half states the truth: I am guarded from what the enemy wants to accomplish in me. In both Psalms 40:1-3 and 40:11, I found I had a responsibility and was to seek and stand on the truth. I am not responsible for the lies and sin that happened to me. But I do have a responsibility to turn toward the truth. At first it seems like very shaky ground, but just as God's voice gets louder and clearer as we listen for and seek Him, so, also, as we obey Him, the ground becomes more of a steadfast place to stand.

के के के

Over time the lies of the enemy became my truth. "God doesn't love you. He has nothing for you. You are not special to Him." Lies become truth when we allow how we are feeling about our circumstances to dictate our perception of reality. *But God has not called me to be the sum of my feelings; I am called to be the sum of His promises!*

God says I am His child and more than a conqueror. The enemy merrily manipulates our feelings. But the truth cannot be manipulated. And truth can be found in God's living Word. Ephesians 2:10 reads, "For we are His creation, created in Christ Jesus for good works, which God prepared ahead of time so that we should walk in them."

God wanted me to learn that saturating myself in the truth and walking in it were not platitudes or the "power of positive thinking." I had walked in the power of lies and deception until it became my reality. They became what I not only believed was the truth but *knew* was the truth, so much so that I *believed* God could heal people and make them whole, but I *knew* from deep in my core that He would not do it for me. My mind and spirit were not healed because His truth had not penetrated me to my core.

MERRY-GO-ROUND

It was the third day of teen camp. Rick and I had to take a quick trip home to sign some documents for a refinance on our house. Some of the other leaders agreed to keep an eye on our younger kids until we got back. The drive home and back gave my husband and me the opportunity to talk privately and uninterrupted about what was happening with me. Rick had been having conversations with the pastor/speaker about me, as well as encouraging me to go talk and pray with him. I told my husband I still wasn't sure I wanted to do that.

Just a few miles into our trip home, I was back to sobbing again. I told my husband this was about my past, and I wasn't sure I was ready for it. Anything that hurt this much couldn't possibly be good for me! He asked me to share with him what I was feeling.

Feeling? Hmm, now there was a question. Let's see: shame, guilt, out of control, but most of all fear. I felt all of these ugly things but did not want to talk to anybody about any of them. I just wanted all these feelings to go back to that safe place I had put them in. I felt … helpless and small and *so* scared. I did not want this to be who I was. I wanted good memories of a wonderful childhood. Restoration seemed impossible. I wanted something back that was gone forever. But most of all I did not want to be that child again!

My husband and I had talked about the things that had

happened to me when I was a little girl. But I had always held some back because I knew it hurt him to hear it as much as it shamed me to tell him. I felt obligated to let him know who I had been, but the few times we spoke about it were so painful for both of us that he told me he didn't need to hear it if I didn't want to repeat it. He wanted badly to be able to protect me and make everything better for me. This arrangement worked, and it wasn't an issue, until now.

As we drove I began to share with Rick all the gruesome details of the abuse I had suffered. I didn't hold anything back this time. I shared every piece of physical abuse they had put me through, every sick game we played. I needed him to hear all of it so it wasn't my ugly secret anymore. It was like lying in bed sick and needing to throw up but forcing yourself not to. Then suddenly you know it's too late, and immediately you are retching out of control.

If he showed disgust at what I shared with him, I knew the disgust was for what had been done to me and not for what I had done. By the end of our long ride home, we had both done a fair share of sobbing. But when we reached our destination, I felt as though a weight had been lifted off of us. It really was like throwing up. It's horrible before it happens, worse while it's occurring, but a massive relief when you are done.

Rick never said anything negative or made me feel guilty for what I shared that day. He still had nothing but love for me. God had dealt with the issue of fault and had been teaching me through my husband and kids about relationship, but I hadn't given up the shame and humiliation. This trip home was a big step in that direction for me.

However, as we got back, I was still apprehensive of what was to come. I told Rick how afraid I was that all the pain I was feeling while I was brought to my knees during chapel was my own. I was terrified it was going to break me into little crumbly pieces. I did not want to revisit anxiety attacks and night terrors or being afraid of the night. I knew I did not want to go back to that dark place. But at the same time, I knew I could not stand still anymore. I could no longer talk myself into believing everything was okay.

ॐॐॐ

Not long after my mom found out about what was happening to my sister and me, she began to get very sick. I think the stress of finding out what had been going on, along with yet another failing marriage, caused her to have a mental breakdown. I remember sitting in the living room of our house and being very sad because I knew she was sick. I wasn't allowed to go into the bedroom and see her because she needed rest and quiet. The grownups around me were saying stuff about her having to leave for a while. I didn't understand why she had to leave when I needed her so much, and she needed me to help her get better. The adults kept telling me "not to worry." But it seemed like I was always afraid and worried. Yes, I was worried. I was really and truly worried.

Right before they took Mom to the hospital, Doug told me about the "mental breakdown." I needed to see her. I needed to see what this "mental breakdown" looked like. I had pictures in my head of all kinds of horrible things that might be wrong with her. I had to make sure she was going to be all right. I had grown used to her leaving, but this time it seemed very different, and I wanted to be allowed to give her a kiss goodbye.

Just before she left, my mother's husband let my sister and me go in and say goodbye. I was surprised at how normal she looked, just tired. She was lying on top of the covers because it was a warm day, and she had all her daytime clothes on. The curtains in the room were open, and the sun was shining in brightly. I remember thinking it wasn't right that she was sick on such a beautiful day. She hugged me and told me she loved me and that she would be back to get us when she was better. Then she left. She went to stay in a hospital, and we were left with Doug. But within the week, we moved out of the house and into his new girlfriend's house. I didn't even know he had a girlfriend!

My world was quickly spinning even faster out of control. I was in shock and trying hard to understand what was happening. A bedroom was all ready for my sister and me at our new house with our new family. But I didn't want a new family. Doug told us we could call this new woman "Mommy." A battle was going on in my head.

Am I supposed to love this mommy? I need a mommy. But I miss my mommy.

As I write this, I am trying to figure out how to convey the absolute turmoil happening inside me at that time. Not only was I living with guilt and shame as part of what I was, but because of the twisted love of some sick people toward me and my acceptance of that love, the blackness that lived as part of me was like something I could touch. Now add to that darkness the guilt of wanting to like Doug's girlfriend. I knew I was betraying my real mommy, and I missed her so much. The whirling was getting faster. I cried out to God, "Help me; please help!"

Doug was a sinister character, even though his new girlfriend was nice. I was terrified at being left with him. After my mom was taken away to the hospital, he told us he wanted to adopt us and raise us as his own. I hated being afraid, and I knew with him there would always be reason to be afraid.

I think of this particular turning point in my childhood as *America's Funniest Home Videos* meets *Nightmare on Elm Street*. There is always that segment in *America's Funniest Home Videos* where there are clips of people spinning on the playground's merry-go-round. At some point they fly off in various unflattering ways, and we all laugh at their folly. We are free to laugh because we know that although those unfortunate victims of the treacherous playground equipment have probably sustained some impressive bruises, they still all got up to walk off their injuries.

In my merry-go-round world, I'm spinning faster and faster, and momentum is pulling with the force of an anvil tied to my small frame. One by one, my fingers are losing their grip on the slippery bars of the whirling metal beast. I know at any moment I won't be able to hold on anymore, and I will be sucked off into blackness where all my fears live. Unlike the people on TV, when I land I will surely shatter into a thousand pieces, as if I were a delicate porcelain doll.

So I was left without my mom. I was left with a man I feared but I wanted to love and trust. And to top it off, there was a new woman I was supposed to call Mommy, or I knew Doug would take out his disappointment in my resistance to her on me. But all I wanted was my real mommy. Even with all the bad things I had experienced up to that time, I had never before felt the kind of despair I felt then.

ॐॐॐ

A few years ago I was sitting in a Sunday morning church service and feeling kind of hopeless about some tough stuff my husband and I were dealing with. The pastor said something about storing up memories of those times when God was faithful to sustain you when it didn't seem He was listening — those times you think He must not care "this time" because you feel so cruddy, and you can't see the sun through the clouds of misery you're experiencing at that moment.

I remember thinking, *Okay, Lord, show me how You have been faithful. I know You have, but I just can't seem to pull any of those memories up to build my faith at the moment.* I waited and sang along with the worship team with as much gusto as I could muster in my sorry state. To my surprise, a ticker tape of blessings started rolling through my mind.

The day my daughter Tiffany gave her life to the Lord … *finally.* The birth of my fifth child and only son. The memory of my husband, on his hands and knees playing with our daughters, wearing a dress-up skirt over his jeans and a homemade princess crown. On and on the ticker tape went, reminding me of how God was always there.

All of us have our own experience of "hopeless" or "alone" and also the fear of what might become of us if despair were allowed to consume us. When I begin to feel hopeless, it reminds me of other times I've felt that way. If I let it, I can spend a whole lot of time in that place, instead of going to the place where I find peace to persevere through trials.

John 16:24 reads, "Ask and you will receive, that your joy may be complete." "That your joy may be complete." I love that part! It is what anyone who has known tragedy and loss desires to experience. Complete joy has no guilt or shame or fear hanging off of it, flapping in the wind like the tail of a kite.

It is such a simple thing. Yet in our weariness we tend to sit in the perceptions which are created by our feelings, instead of going straight to the one in whom we find our peace and strength. "But those who trust in the Lord will renew their strength; they will soar on wings like eagles; they will run and not grow weary; they will walk and not faint" (Isaiah 40:31). That sounds like complete joy to me.

REPRIEVE

"Why weren't You there, Lord? I can't see You there. How can I love You when I can't remember Your presence when I needed You most? God?" I could not bring myself to call Him "Father." He was too distant to my mind. He sat up in heaven and watched and judged, waiting for me to break. But I had learned to be strong and self-sufficient. No mom, no dad, no adult and no god had saved me from the terror. I had been brought to the very edge of my breaking point in the past, but I had always been able to pull myself back.

❧❧❧

As another night of chapel commences, the pressure of what my heart wants to believe about the God I have chosen to give my life to and what my mind *actually* believes is weighing heavily on me. I may fool everyone else, but He has not been fooled.

I feel like a sponge being rung out into the sink as every tear I have refused to cry is now being wrenched from me. I know what He wants from me, but I don't know how to give it. He wants me to reconcile who He truly is. Either God is God (and *all* His Word says He is), or God is defined by me and the sum of all my feelings. He cannot and will not be both.

As I kneel on the chapel floor, I am begging the Lord to show me who He is. "Show me that You loved me then, so I can love You now."

∂∂∂

My sister and I stayed with Doug and his girlfriend for a few months. Or maybe it was only a few weeks, I don't really remember. My mother's parents wanted my sister and me until my mom could take care of us again. Doug actually went to court to fight to retain custody of us.

I clearly recall the night before my grandparents would go to court against our current stepfather to decide who would have temporary custody of my sister and me. Doug asked me to come and talk to him. It was late, and he and his girlfriend were lying in bed. He asked me if I wanted to stay with him because he was willing to fight for us to stay with him.

I knew I was supposed to say yes. I knew that if I didn't he would be very angry at me. But I just couldn't bring myself to lie and say what he wanted to hear from me. I don't know how I mustered the strength, but I knew for certain that I wasn't really safe there with him, and I wanted to be away from him badly.

When the defiant truth was what came out of my mouth, instead of what he wanted to hear, he gave me a stony look. "Fine," he said, "I won't even try." I went to bed that night feeling guilty and sick about what might happen in the courtroom the next day. The merry-go-round was spinning faster and faster, and I just wanted to get off.

It took one day. A few short minutes in front of a judge and my grandparents had temporary custody of my sister and me. That very day our clothes were packed, and we were taken to yet another new home.

When I was a little girl, my mom's mother and stepfather were my favorite people in the world. Whenever we would go to visit them, they would both be standing on their front porch as we pulled up to their house. Their arms would be spread wide, ready to receive my greedy hugs. I always loved our infrequent visits to Grandma and Grandpa's house. For me, there was a feeling of warmth there I didn't find anywhere else.

As soon as my sister and I arrived at their house to stay for good I felt safe and loved. It is the only time in my childhood that I remember feeling truly at ease. They had prepared a pretty bedroom for us to share. There was a cozy double bed where my sister and I would sleep together and a sweet little vanity with a mirror above it. I loved the vanity. It always made me feel like a princess sitting in the dainty little chair, looking at my reflection.

The best way I can describe how I felt being there would be to liken it to my ideal little girl dollhouse. I had always loved those beautiful dollhouses that would open in the back so you could reach in and move around the happy miniature family who lived there into different poses. I never actually owned one, but I had always dreamed of having one, and I would have kept it in the most brilliant condition. In my dollhouse, everyone is happy and content, and it's always warm and tidy inside. Nobody scary ever visits, and the highlight of every day is when the sun is setting and everyone you love is sitting around the dinner table with you discussing the important events of the day.

In the short time I was able to spend with my grandma and grandpa, I developed in my heart a picture of what I wanted to achieve in my life. I wanted peace, security and consistency. I didn't know how to quantify it then, or even how to put it into words, but looking back I knew what my grandparents had: peace, security and consistency. I wanted warm food every night and church on Sundays. I knew even at that young age security and order would always be something I would strive for.

For me, my grandparents' house was a wonderful respite. I loved crawling into bed with them on Saturday mornings. On those mornings, when we would finally get out of bed, Grandma would make us pancakes and gravy, and my sister and I would have a pancake-eating contest with Grandpa. Dinner was always at the dining room table with a napkin folded beside your dinner plate.

Grandma was a wonderful cook to my young appetite. I loved that there was always plenty to eat, and it was always tasty and fresh. We had vegetables straight out of Grandpa's garden and plenty of fresh fruit. I remember we always had a small plate of celery to eat with every dinner. My grandma said it was good for digestion. Even though it wasn't my favorite, I didn't question her wisdom. It was all those sorts of simple consistencies, celery with dinner, pancakes on Saturday mornings and church on Sundays, that helped me to feel safe and secure.

Grandma and Grandpa lived on a 25-acre farm surrounded by woods and fields to play in and explore. My only cause for sadness at my grandparents' house was that my sister was not as happy there as I was. Well, there was that and the fact that my mom didn't live there with us.

My sister had become very rebellious and would often get mad about the boundaries my grandparents set. She would take off out our bedroom window into the woods that surrounded the house. She even did this at night a few times. I remember waiting anxiously for them to find her and bring her back safely.

Aside from my mom, my sister was the most important person in the world to me. She had always been my best friend, and it made me sad that she wouldn't be good so I wouldn't have to see her get into trouble. I wanted us to just have fun together and get along with Grandma and Grandpa. We had lived in so many scary places with so many scary people, I desperately wanted her and I to be able to stay in a place where I could fall asleep knowing I would be safe throughout the night.

We stayed with my grandparents for about a year. It was the best year of my childhood. It was like the calm in the storm of my young life, and it ended far too soon.

My biological father found my sister and me and wanted us to live with him. Throughout the time I lived at my grandparents, my mom had been coming for visits after she got out of the hospital. She seemed to me to be doing quite well, and I would rather have gone back with her. But she said she wasn't ready, and we should give our real dad a chance. I was more than a little anxious at the start of yet another life with another family I didn't know.

෨෨෨

It amazes me now to see how I have allowed the Lord access to my heart. He is a good and faithful Father. For so long, I had been so sure in my disappointment and sorrow at the Lord, convinced that He had not been there for me when I cried out to Him. I spent years asking Him, "Why? Why didn't You help me?" I couldn't understand how I could reconcile the Jesus that I knew had suffered immensely to save me with the God who had, in my eyes, abandoned me. I just couldn't bring these two figures together into one. I think I had learned to concentrate on Jesus and just try to ignore God.

Not too long ago, my husband and I had a conversation about why bad things happen to good people, especially to innocent children. I had asked the Lord relentlessly why He had allowed people to hurt me. My husband explained it in this way.

God gave all His children free will so that they might choose to be in a relationship with Him. If I have no choice to be in a relationship and no free choice within that relationship, then it is slavery. God did not create us to be slaves. Instead He wants us to love and worship Him simply because He is worth loving.

I am made in His image, therefore, I desire relationship and to be loved as well. For instance, I want my husband to love me because I am worth loving, not for what I do or don't do for him. I don't want him to love me out of obligation simply because divorce is too costly and miserable. I am made for relationship, and I am made to give love and be loved.

With free will comes great freedom. Freedom to choose righteousness or to choose evil. Freedom to loose and freedom to bind. Freedom to bring life or to bring death. Our free will has great consequences for us as individuals and for those around us. Throughout history, whole nations have suffered at the hands of individual leaders' evil decisions. Innocent people suffer the consequences of selfish, self-serving and evil choices. If an evil man chooses to hurt a child and God intervenes, how many times must God intervene before we would say that he (the evil person) no longer has free will? God will not contradict Himself. At times, God will intervene, and we do experience His providence. Other times, we suffer.

But what I came to realize is that He has always promised healing! It was not that God did not come to my rescue because of a lack of love or desire. He made me in my mother's womb and had a plan for my life from the beginning of creation. But because of my parents' continuous poor choices, I suffered. The abuse is not what I was created for. But God made a way for me to find healing, to find that love that only comes through true relationship, to find Him.

As I lay there on the chapel floor, God was showing me He had seen all of the pain I had suffered. He felt the betrayal I had felt. Most importantly, He was showing me that I was His, and He would see accomplished in me what He had planned for me. God and His plans were not limited in my life because of what was done to me.

Having this epiphany catapulted me toward healing and wholeness, toward getting back what Satan had tried to steal. I can now look back and see God's hand on my life, calling me and protecting me. God says He will restore what the locust destroyed (Joel 2:25).

The Lord's answers to my questions may not have come in the way I thought they would, the way I thought they should or even when I thought they must. This brings me to another area that was crucial to my process of healing. Just because God does not answer the way I think He should, it does not make Him wrong or mean. The best way I can think of to explain this is to use my 8-year-old son.

When he comes to me and asks for something and I don't think I should allow it, I will generally try and explain myself. If he still does not understand, I will often try and explain it again. If he still does not understand or even disagrees with my choice, am I any less right due to his lack of understanding?

When I don't understand the Lord, or I disagree with what He is allowing in my life, is He any less right or do I just not understand? If I hope for this kind of maturity to be developed in my children, shouldn't I strive to see the Holy Spirit develop it in me? Longsuffering is one of the nine fruits of the Spirit.

FUTURE GENERATIONS

By evening of day three, I am starting to accept that this wretched, desperate pain is all mine, and the years of tears I have held onto must be given to the One who died for me. I knew I had to keep moving forward in this place the Lord had brought me to. It was not by mistake that I was at this camp where the pastor was speaking each night about the horrors of abuse and how the enemy wants us destroyed from the moment we are conceived. It was not by chance but by God's providence that I would be here to finally deal with what had been stolen from me.

On this particular night, as I am again sobbing on the floor, my daughter Ryleigh has been watching me. Her concern for me had reached a point where she was very upset. As I wrote earlier, she had never witnessed me cry or seem so miserable. She went to one of the pastors and asked him what she could do for me or how she could help me. He told her to go and pray that the Lord would show her. So she went back to her seat to pray for a while. After a little while, she came and put her arms around me as I knelt on the floor. She just sat there and hugged me and rubbed my back, trying to give me comfort. After a few minutes she leaned into my ear and said, "You are the best mommy ever! No one would ever know what you went through growing up by looking at you now. I love you." Then she got up and went away to pray again.

I can't tell you what it meant to me to hear that from her. I always wanted my children to feel that they were cherished and special, and for her to say that to me told me I had been successful in that. Her words opened a whole new floodgate of emotions for me. My three older daughters knew sketchy details of my past. We had to tell them something over the years when they began to ask why they didn't know their grandfather (my dad) or why they couldn't ever go stay with my mom.

Ryleigh returned to my side a few minutes later and put her arms around me again. She leaned in and said, "Thank you, Mommy, for going through all of that so I don't have to." That was it! At that moment I knew I would have suffered through 10 lifetimes like the one I had to spare my children the pain I had endured. Every day I watched my kids grow — loved and safe and full of the joy of childhood — had brought me closer to a place of full healing. It healed my heart to see my husband loving his kids the way God had intended a father to love his children. The process of healing in my life wasn't as quick as I wanted, but it was speeding up.

☙☙☙

My dad showed up at my grandparents' house in an old red pickup truck. He had his third wife and her two young daughters with him. This was before seatbelt laws, and they had arrived in a single-cab truck, so the four of them were crammed into the front together. After quick introductions and a sad goodbye to my grandparents, my sister's and my stuff was loaded into the bed of the truck. We all squished into the cab like sardines in a can, and off my sister and I went to our new home. Since my two new stepsisters were the smallest (they were just 3 and 4 at the time), they sat on the floor of the truck, and my sister and I sat between my dad and his wife. It was very cramped conditions for a long car ride and even more so considering I didn't know these people.

It was about an hour drive from my grandparents' house to the small rickety house we would be calling home. I remember it was in a very rundown neighborhood, and our house seemed to be one of the worst. Later I would find out we actually did live in one of the worst parts of Tacoma. I knew it was pretty bad because my friends from school weren't allowed to come to my house. I had to go to theirs instead. My dad's house had dingy beige-colored siding that felt like sandpaper and a steep rock garden as the front yard. I remember thinking, *Who plants rocks?*

The downstairs consisted of a small living room leading to a combination kitchen/dining room, then a bathroom that led to the small laundry room. Upstairs were three bedrooms, with no hallway. Just walk right on through one bedroom to get to the next! I had never lived in a house without a hallway before.

And no carpet! Nowhere in the whole house was there any carpet! I thought it was the strangest house. The middle bedroom didn't even have a window, just doorways connecting to the other two bedrooms on either end.

The worst part to me was the mess. Everywhere in this house was messy and smelled of potting soil. It was quite a shock to go from the cozy hominess of Grandma's house to this place, where the upstairs floors were only the plywood floorboards rather than the comfy carpet I used to stretch out on. This may seem strange, but one thing I've always liked about my mom was no matter where we lived or how simple, it was always picked up. My mom was always very tidy and still is.

However, things at my dad's house seemed to go along fine for a while. We had a large backyard to play in with an old rickety swing set and a garden. There were also lots of kids in the neighborhood, so we always had playmates. It was summer, so my dad's wife would send the four of us out just after breakfast, and we weren't allowed back in until dinnertime. Lunch was served outside at the picnic table.

I didn't mind having to stay outside because there was always something to do. We lived near a gulch and would go exploring there or play down in the "Lower Forty." This was actually just the lower part of our backyard, which was infested with overgrown blackberry bushes. But they called it the Lower Forty. Not really sure where the name came from, probably a farming term, but it stuck.

My dad was an electrician for a large aerospace company, so we lived comfortably enough. In fact, now that I am an adult, I don't really understand why he lived in such a rundown house in a horrible area of town. My father grew up an underprivileged first-generation Mexican. Maybe he had become used to bad neighborhoods and poor living conditions.

On weekends we camped a lot or spent time at a nearby lake. Often in the evenings we would go to the drive-in theater. For me, this was never much fun. My dad and his wife only liked horror movies. So that was the only kind of movie we ever went to.

We would arrive at the drive-in early to get a good spot and then get to go play on the playground for 30 or 40 minutes before the movie started. Then it was back to the car to see how far I could shove my fingers into my ears to block out the scary music pumped in through the window-mounted speaker. It never helped. I could always still hear the screams and sinister music from whatever evil movie was the pick of the week.

That first summer we came to live with my dad, we took a road trip to Arizona to meet his family. He and his wife had bought a brand-spanking-new AMC Gremlin that summer. (That's correct: They made payments … on a Gremlin.) Since the Gremlin was more reliable than the old red pickup, we strapped the luggage to the top, crammed all six of us into it (including one child in the hatchback area) and headed off to Arizona.

We stayed with my dad's mom and dad for most of our stay. My dad is from a very large family, and I don't remember much about all the different people I met. I do remember, though, that many of them didn't speak

English. I also remember it was very exciting knowing I was part of such a large family.

My grandfather was one of the family who did not speak any English. He seemed ancient to me with his weathered, dark skin. On one occasion, he gestured to me to follow him to one of the back rooms. Warning bells were going off in my head. But at that time, one of the ways I dealt with people who were scary but had the control was to act passively in the hope it would be over quickly. I felt if I was nice and accommodating, they would be kind enough not to hurt me violently. Most of the time it worked.

I followed my grandfather to a bedroom and sat down on the bed as he instructed me. I couldn't understand what he was saying to me, but he was giving me a jar of candy or something while he was speaking. As he was trying to persuade me to accept whatever gift he was offering, he was rubbing my back and legs.

It was hot that day, so I was wearing shorts and a halter top. I could feel his callused fingers intimately massaging my bare skin. As his fingers crept further and further up my leg, I knew I had to escape. I clutched the jar of candy to my chest, slid off the bed and ran out of the room without a backward look. For the rest of our time there, I pretended not to understand my grandfather when he tried to get my attention. I was relieved when time finally came for us to head back home, but the fear and the whirling were increasing again.

We took a few days to get home, staying in hotels at

night. On the first night, it was again sweltering. The room had no air conditioning, so my dad told all us girls to sleep in our underpants.

My dad's wife had gone to the store for some snacks, so we were left to watch TV with my dad. He asked my older sister to come sit down on the floor next to him, while the rest of us stayed on the bed. There were two beds, and the TV was on the wall directly at the foot of the beds. My dad and my sister were directly at the foot of the bed. My other sisters and I were lying down, so we couldn't really see them from our prone position.

I remember being a little jealous that he had chosen her to cuddle with and not me. A few days after we got home from our vacation, my sister told me that our dad had been touching her "down there" while they were on the floor. I felt that familiar weary anticipation. Yep, I was back on the merry-go-round. It was definitely starting to spin again.

It didn't take my dad long to start laying the foundation for what I knew was to come. It started with longer kisses on the mouth when he would say goodnight and progressed to his being casually sprawled naked across his bed for me to see as I passed through his room to mine. Often he would be laying across his bed naked asking for a hug and kiss goodnight, and I would have to passively agree.

One night, while his wife was downstairs watching TV and the other girls had fallen asleep, my dad crept into the room I shared with my sister. He lay down on the bed with me. He told me, as my father, he had the responsibility to get me ready for the boys I would date when I was 16. I remember that number stuck in my head. *Sixteen*. Why 16? Was it the magic "have sex with your boyfriend" number? By the time he came to my room, I knew that it was inevitable. I was sad, afraid and, by this time, also angry. But most of all I was tired, so deeply weary I just wanted to sleep forever without interruption. I didn't care about him. I didn't care about me. I just wanted to sleep and not have to endure late-night "lessons."

From that night on, I slept with my sister in her bed. He came in our room a few nights later, and I rolled toward my sister and put an arm and a leg over her as she slept. I told him, "NO!" I had no idea where the strength to utter those words came from. I told him he had to get out of our room, and to my surprise and utter relief, he did.

ॐ ॐ ॐ

When I started preparing to write this book, I took a lot of time to think about the sequence of events at that time in my life. Something I was starting to see was that my dad must have been aware he would be found out. He knew all about what had happened to my sister and me. I think that's how he got custody from my mom.

I believe he must have known my sister had told on the people that were abusing us. He had to have realized we would tell again. Why would he choose to take that kind of a risk? Also, he hadn't touched any of us before that trip home to see his family. I remember him telling us he hadn't seen his parents in many years. After the trip to see his father, he escalated quickly to abusing us, almost like seeing his father was a trigger.

I would assume that my dad, as well as his brothers and sisters, had also been molested by their father based on how my grandfather behaved with me. Sin is always ugly and always leads to death. But generational sin is especially ugly. God hates sin because it separates us from Him.

Generational sin separates not only from relationship with God, but also relationships within families.

I've done some research into generational sin as the Lord has been bringing me through the process of restoration. I have five children, as I have mentioned, so this topic is of great importance to me. I want myself, as well as all the generations that come from me, to be free from the garbage I have endured.

One of the best explanations I have found was in an article printed by *Restoring Your Life Ministries*. The article describes generational sin as a spiritual pressure to commit the same sins your parents or grandparents committed. Deuteronomy 5:9-10 reads, "I, the Lord your God, am a jealous God, punishing the children for the father's sin to the third and fourth generations of those who hate Me, but showing faithful love to a thousand generations of those who love Me and keep My commands." The article goes on to talk about the need for us to break the cycle of sin by acknowledging the sins of past generations, confessing them and asking for forgiveness so that you can be free of those spiritual pressures.

Leviticus 26:40-42 reads, "But if they will confess their sins and the sins of their fathers — their unfaithfulness that they practiced against Me, and I acted with hostility toward them and brought them into the land of their enemies — and if their uncircumcised hearts will be humbled, and if they will pay the penalty of their sin, then I will remember My covenant with Jacob. I will also remember My covenant with Isaac and My covenant with Abraham, and I will remember the land." Jesus paid for everything when He hung on the cross, but just as we must ask for and receive our salvation, we must also receive our freedom from the corruption of sin. In doing this, you not only free yourself, but also the generations that come from you.

My daughter Ryleigh had a divine revelation about generational sin and how it could have ultimately affected her if I hadn't taken action. That action was to receive Christ as my Savior, to acknowledge the sin in my life and bring it into the light.

"Christ has redeemed us from the curse of the law by becoming a curse for us, because it is written: Cursed is everyone who is hung on a tree" (Galatians 3:13).

BREAKING CHAINS

Ryleigh's whispered words to me seemed to open a door into my heart. God had changed my life's legacy and had saved my children from a generational cycle. The truth always pierces the darkness. I realized that even if I never moved beyond the depth with the Lord I was at when I came to camp that year, I would still be forever grateful for all His blessings and for knowing Him at all. When she said those words to me, I knew they were straight out of God's mouth. He knew me. He had always known me and was always there. He just wasn't finished with me yet.

I had experienced so much disappointment in my life as a young girl that I had let it become my interpretation of God. "The Almighty Disappointer." How many times had I hoped in Him and been disappointed? I realized it was my choice if I was going to trust Him or not. What if I never got to understand? One thing was becoming clear to me: I desired a type of intimacy with a father that I had never known.

The time I was spending weeping on the floor with the Lord was not because I was angry with Him. Even though it was uncomfortable being so vulnerable, I was closer to Him than I had ever felt. I wanted to unload on Him every desperate moment I had ever experienced so I could be free of it. He was telling my heart, *I'll take it. My shoulders*

*are as broad as the ocean is wide, and no burden is too
heavy.*

By the end of the fourth night, I was able to stay in the
actual service without feeling totally stricken with fear and
physically ill. The pastor was speaking about forgiveness. I
consider myself a reasonably smart individual, and I knew
enough about the Bible to know it said if you don't
forgive, you won't be forgiven. So, of course, I had already
forgiven all those who had wronged me. I knew I had
mostly done it out of obedience. But I figured, *What more
could You expect of me? I mean, look what had been done
to me.*

The pastor, Daren, took us all through an exercise in
forgiveness. He started by instructing us to receive the
forgiveness that Jesus bought for us on the cross. When
Jesus went to the cross, He did it as the payment for all sin,
even sins not yet committed by anybody. So I closed my
eyes and received His forgiveness. Next we were to picture
in front of us a person we felt had sinned against us. We
were to picture that person bound at the wrists by a lash
that was our unforgiveness toward them. The person who
popped into my head was my father. *Why him?* I thought.
*I've already forgiven him. I even told him I forgave him
for everything.*

In my early 20s, I drove to my father's house and told
him that I wanted to forgive him for what he had done to
me. His response to me was, "I paid my penance (he is
Catholic) and have already forgiven myself for that, so it's
over and done with." Okay. So maybe that wasn't the

reaction I had hoped for. But I had not done it for him. I had done it for me.

༺ ༺ ༺

After that second night when my dad came to our room and I told him to leave, he didn't come back again. I didn't know at the time whether he would return or not, so my sleep was never sound. There was always the dread that he would try again, and what if I wasn't strong enough to make him leave the next time?

I was desperately disappointed in how this relationship between my dad and I had turned out. I hadn't realized how much hope I had put into this person, my dad. One of my only memories of him before we came to live with him was a visit when I was about 3 years old. He picked my sister and me up in an old green car, and we drove to the ferry docks. I remember being a little scared because I didn't really know him. But he smiled at me a lot and bought me a cookie. He asked my sister for a bite of hers, so she broke off the smallest crumb and handed it to him. He laughed and laughed at her stinginess. It was so exciting to get to take the short ferry ride to wherever it was that he lived. I don't remember much more than that about that weekend. But the impression I had always kept was that he was fun and seemed to like us.

I was relieved when school started that first year at his house. I was entering fourth grade, and I had always really enjoyed school. I was looking forward to getting away from the house that was so tainted with the shadow of misery that the shadow seemed to follow me from room to room.

The "uncle" my sister had told on was in the process of being prosecuted for his crimes against us and some of the other children he had victimized. As a result, the courts suggested that we speak with a school counselor once a week to assure that we were recovering from the whole mess. So every week I went into the office of the nice lady, wanting to tell her about my dad. But I didn't.

My sister and I were seeing our mom every other weekend, and we had decided together that we would tell her about the abuse on one of our visits. We figured that way she would keep us with her where we would be safe from anyone ever trying to hurt us again. So weekend after weekend we went to see her, and every time we decided to tell her, we would wait till next time.

I think down deep we were afraid that the information might make her "sick" again. So we kept waiting. Finally I couldn't keep the secret anymore. Without telling my sister first, I told the nice lady I talked with each week at school what my dad had done.

Everything went crazy after that. Back on the merry-go-round I went. The counselor sent for my sister, and the police were called. When my sister came in, I could tell she was fuming mad at me for telling. We had had a plan, and I had messed it up. The police went straight to my house and picked up my two little sisters, then came to the school to get us. We were all driven away in the back of police cars, while the other students were just coming out to get on their buses for home. I was incredibly humiliated, my sister was ticked and the two younger ones were excited to be riding in the cool police car.

I was wondering if they had called my mom or maybe my grandma. I was hoping that would be where we would be going next. I desperately wanted to be with my mother, but I would settle for the peace and safety of my grandma's.

The police officers took us straight to a foster home. I was so confused and disappointed. Why hadn't they called my mom? She would want us to come straight to her so she could protect us from my dad. I felt incredibly guilty about jumping the gun and ruining our plan to be with our mother.

The four of us only stayed with the foster family for three days while Dad was removed from our home. We were then taken back to our dingy beige house. Apparently the police had arrested my dad while he was at his job. His crime was a felony, and felons didn't get to work at the company he was working for, so he was fired immediately (or at least I was told my dad lost his job because of me). I don't think he ever served any jail time.

When the social workers returned us home, our camping trailer was gone. My stepmom said Dad had taken it and was living in it elsewhere until things were worked out. When I was finally allowed to talk to my mom, she said she didn't have custody anymore, so there was no way she could get us back without hiring a lawyer and fighting my dad for us. She said she was sorry, but she just didn't have the money for a lawyer. But she said she would "work on it."

A few weeks later my dad moved back in. He gave a tearful apology and installed a court-ordered lock on the door between his room and ours. We were instructed to lock the door after retiring to our room for the night. Oh, and he was no longer allowed to kiss us on the mouth at bedtime, only kisses on the cheek. Problem solved, right?

That time in my life was what I felt was my descent into darkness. My hope and belief that anything good and safe was in any way sustainable was gone. I had thought by telling on my dad I would be safe from him. I felt betrayed now, not only by the grownups who were supposed to care for me, but also by the entire judicial system. I was often reminded by my stepmom that the reason we had no money was because I had cost my dad his job. I felt trapped and alone. The only person I could really ever count on at all was my sister, and she was angry that I had messed up our chances of being with our mom. The depth of sadness I felt seemed like a bottomless pit.

It was then that fear began to be my constant companion. I know I've written that as a small child I was always afraid. That's true. But the difference now was that I quit calling out to God, I quit hoping to be saved, I quit believing life could ever be good. It was like every fear or dread I had ever experienced up to that point had been wadded up to attack me all at once with absolutely no hope of escape.

I was so filled with fear I was afraid of being afraid. I was afraid of nighttime, the dark, being in a room by myself and a number of other things. I was afraid to close my eyes as I lay down to go to sleep and afraid to keep them open. I was afraid of everything and nothing. My fears were so irrational, and though I see that now, back then I just thought I was crazy.

I couldn't even free myself with sleep because my dreams were never anything to look forward to. I would have the craziest nightmares, and many of them I would have again and again.

I would dream of being relentlessly pursued by faceless monsters through quicksand, watching myself being filleted open with an ax, knowing I should be dead but for some reason living with the mortal wound. Or witnessing the sky darken with alien ships I knew would destroy the earth.

I experienced endless panic attacks and night terrors. The worst was when my fear and anxiety would ease up a bit and I would start to have hope that I was going to finally be okay. Then something would trigger all the garbage, and I would be plunged right back into the pit of torment.

It's difficult for people who have never suffered from depression or anxiety to understand, and I find it difficult even to explain. The best way I can describe it is like living under constant overcast skies, like someone had put a gray lens on the camera that photographed my world. I could laugh and have fun, but it was always tainted with the dread of what I knew was inevitable; the fear was always lurking right around the bend to consume me at any moment of its choosing.

That sense of depression was with me throughout my teen years. And it came rushing back to me when the pastor said, "Picture in your mind the person you want to offer forgiveness to." Until that moment, I hadn't realized how much my dad had hurt me. He was my hope of what a father might be. The men my mom had married hadn't been that to me. The other men who had touched me wrongly hadn't been that to me. My dad had only touched me wrongly one time, but in that moment he had ruined everything precious attached to the word "father." I could not call the God I was supposed to love "father."

The exercise went on. Pastor Daren explained how sometimes we have been wronged so horribly that it seems impossible to forgive. We just don't have it in ourselves to forgive what is unforgivable. But by receiving forgiveness from the Lord, it is now in us to give away. "Now," the pastor said, "picture you removing the lash from that person's wrists." He used the word "unloose." He explained that the person in front of us was bound by our judgment. He asked us to take the imaginary lash of judgment and hold it up in front of us. The speaker then told us to make a proclamation before God. "In Jesus' name, I forgive you." And then the exercise got really hard.

"Now," he went on, "think of three things you would like the Lord to bless you with." It could be anything:

wealth, a new car, a healthy life, whatever we desired. The next part was shocking to me. He asked us to ask the Lord to bless the person we had just forgiven with those three things we most wanted for ourselves. *Wow,* I thought, *he tricked us!*

As I spoke those blessings from my heart for my dad, something in me broke. I felt the Lord speak to my heart: *This is how I forgive.* Jesus doesn't just forgive. He forgives and blesses. The memory of the abuse by my dad had tormented me my whole life. The pastor warned us that the enemy would no doubt try to push the "play button" on the memory to try and get the same ugly reactions, feelings of hate and unforgiveness. Our defense was to go straight back to blessing that person again. Blessings are the opposite of what the enemy wants to accomplish, so eventually he will stop pushing the button.

The first time I forgave my dad, I had done it out of obedience. It was like when I tell my kids they had to say they're sorry when they are mean to one another. I know, at that moment, they aren't sorry at all. But the right thing to do is to say the words. Then the wronged sibling would have to say, "I forgive you," in return. My hope was as they said the words with their mouths, eventually their hearts would follow, especially after they saw that once their sibling was appeased, they could both go on to play again and have fun.

I realized that the first time I had offered my dad forgiveness, it had been with strings attached. When his response was not what I had wanted, I took the forgiveness back. I held onto all the pain and anguish he had created in me, and I held it against him.

Hate and anger are emotions we think we can control. I can hold them and mold them. I cannot control whether you love me. I could not control my dad's response. But if I put him back in the box I had made for him, I could control him.

It is easy to hate someone who doesn't do what you want. How many times do we sin and then go to God and ask for forgiveness, only to go out and commit the same sin again? How many times does God forgive us and we don't respond back the way we should? But God, in His infinite grace, forgives us again and again and blesses us in spite of our not deserving it. "As far as the east is from the west, so far has He removed our transgressions from us" (Psalm 103:12). He does not remember, and He does not hold it against us. He never takes His forgiveness back. He blesses His children instead!

As I saw myself blessing my dad, I was blessed so much more. Another door in my heart was opened, emptied out and left ready to be filled.

A side note in regard to hate: By hating my father and not forgiving him, I was allowing him to re-victimize me over and over. By the time of camp, my father had been out of my life for many years. But the hate I held in kept him with me always. My hate kept me bound in all the garbage I was so desperately trying to pretend I no longer carried with me.

RESTORATION, NOT JUSTIFICATION

By the fifth night, I found myself looking forward to the smelly chapel floor. It was becoming my refuge. I had an excited anticipation about the time the Lord would bring me to my knees. My heart was starting to see this Lord of Hosts in a whole new light. As I poured out all of my stored-up grief at His feet, I was beginning to see Him as the "Mighty Counselor," rather than the "mighty disappointer" I had previously labeled Him.

For so many years, I had sung the worship songs at the beginning of the service not believing the words I recited were true. I didn't want "the rocks to cry out." Seriously, I would often offer my worship for the same reason I had offered my father forgiveness — because I was supposed to. I now see that I responded to my Heavenly Father the way I did to my earthly father. I gave what I thought I was supposed to give out of obligation, not love.

Knowing this caused such desperation in my soul. The Holy Spirit urged me to sing the words, but it was not out of adoration; it was out of obedience.

For a while, obedience worked for me. But as I watched the relationship my husband had with our children and their complete and utter trust in him, I began to desire more from my relationship with my Father in heaven. I wanted to trust God like I saw my children trust their daddy.

He could throw them high into the air with his strong arms, and there was never a trace of anything other than complete joy on their faces as they fell back to his waiting embrace. They would often wait by the door when it was time for him to come home from work, totally excited to see him and have him hug or play with them. I desperately wanted to love God with the reckless abandon and anticipation I saw my kids have for their daddy.

I would read Psalm 40:11-13 so often the binding is worn to automatically open to the page. It reads, "Lord, do not withhold Your compassion from me; Your constant love and truth will always guard me. For troubles without number have surrounded me; my sins have overtaken me; I am unable to see. They are more than the hairs of my head, and my courage leaves me. Lord, be pleased to deliver me; hurry to help me, Lord."

I so desired for the Lord to deliver me, like He had delivered His servant, David. Even in my unbelief the Lord desired to meet me where I was. He was now bringing me to a place where it was just He and I. As I sang the words of worship out of obedience to the Holy Spirit and searched His Word for proof of who He was, the Lord brought me to a place where He could show me.

ॐॐॐ

After my dad had so completely let me down, I began to live for the weekends I would be allowed to visit my mom. All the days in between our visits were just time spent in anticipation of the weekend when I could be with her. Even with all that had occurred, I still had a deep love for my mom.

It was the late 70s, so due to trouble with the Middle East, the United States was in the midst of a gas crisis. Gas lines were long, due to oil and gasoline being rationed. I didn't mind sitting in the gas lines, even when they would sometimes take an hour or more. I knew the reward for the boredom would be almost two whole days with my mom.

When I was with her none of the fears and anxiety that plagued me at my dad's house followed me. I looked forward to everything about being with her.

Once I got over the fact that she would not be able to take us because of all the legal costs, I completely believed it wasn't her fault. I lived for the time we could be together.

She would always plan fun things for us to do: the zoo, parks, movies. Of course, I wouldn't have cared if all we did was sit in her small apartment and watch television together. As long as I was with her, I was content. When I was with her I could sleep with my head out of the covers — unlike at home, where I would tuck myself in tightly like a human burrito with just a small air hole and wait for my brain to turn off enough to sleep.

Being with my mother was where the veil of shadow was lifted off of me, and the world was a bright and happy place to live. I put every bit of hope and faith I had left into the dream of one day being able to be with her always, not just every other weekend. She was the only dim light in my otherwise dark world.

I still felt guilty about jumping the gun when I blew the whistle on my dad. I knew for certain if I had been with her when I told, she would never have sent me back to him. It was the screwed-up court system's fault. My dad had custody, and he was not willing to give it up without a fight. My mom said it was because he knew he would be saddled with child support, and up until that time, he had never paid any. She said he was not about to have to start paying it now. Every time my sister and I would cry for him to let us go live with Mom, he would pull out those cursed custody papers and waive them in our faces, bellowing about how he was the only one who had even wanted us.

Weekends with my mom were always like one of Shakespeare's tragedies, wonderful at first with the promise of ending badly. I knew Sunday at five o'clock would come, and I would be on my way back to the darkness of reality. The ride home was especially painful. I would sit in the backseat and pretend to be asleep with my head turned to the door so no one would see the tears rolling down my cheeks. The radio would be playing top 40s or soft rock (my mom's favorite), and I would be miserable wondering why I wasn't allowed to be happy for more than two days at a time.

I didn't understand why my dad would not want to just give us back. My sister and I did not get along with his wife. We fought constantly against her authority over us.

My sister especially would go to battle with her, just like she had at our grandparents' house. I remember one battle where my sister ended up having her face held under running water in the sink by my dad's wife until she would agree to stop screaming. I suppose it was her version of water boarding. I would have thought my dad's wife would have realized she was only causing my sister to scream louder.

With every fight I thought, *This time, for sure, they will send us to Mom. They don't even like us.* But every time, out would come the custody papers to remind us of my dad's ultimate power over our world. I hated them both and resigned myself to wait for the weekends where I would have a brief time of peace.

Our family attended weekly counseling sessions for a long time after the sexual abuse came out. I believe it was ordered by the court as part of my dad's sentence. I think he also had to go to sessions on his own and Alcoholics Anonymous meetings as well. All the counseling just seemed to make my dad more resentful of what I had done to him. And the only thing this experience with the courts did for me was convince me not to say anything to a counselor.

Our family counselor told us we needed to have weekly family meetings at our home, in addition to the group sessions we had with her. There was no third-party mediating. The idea was we would have a safe place to discuss issues with no threat of retaliation. The only good thing that came out of those ridiculous meetings was the ice cream and cookies I got when they were over (also suggested by the counselor).

The counselor also told my parents to discontinue taking their young children to horror movies. I guess my dad was strongly encouraged by the courts to listen to all advice given by the court-appointed counselor, because her suggestions always became law at our house. For me, no more horror movies came with good and bad consequences. On the one hand, I was spared having to endure the movies and the awful nightmares that would come after them. On the other hand, it was just more fuel for my young stepmother's resentment of my sister and me. Because we were too young to stay home by ourselves and too poor to hire a babysitter (since I had cost my father his good job and now no one would hire him), one of her favorite things to do for fun was out.

Regardless of all the counseling sessions we attended, as a whole we were one very dysfunctional unit. Of course, at that time, I didn't recognize just how dysfunctional we were.

After a time of nothing getting better, I just stopped expecting it to. But as the next few years went on with just more of the same, I started to question why my mom didn't try harder to get us back. My sister got more and more rebellious, acting out by running away for days at a time. I turned more and more inward, finding peace in being by myself when I had to be at home. As much as possible, I threw myself into things outside of my family, like sports, music and school. I strove to be the best at everything I tried: A grades, first chair in choir and the funniest of all my friends.

But my hope in my mom was fading, and the joy I felt when I was with her wasn't enough to sustain me anymore. I was getting the sense when I was with her that something had been lost and would never be found again. I had the sense I was running out of time, just like when the alien ships were hovering above my head in my dreams. All hope was lost, and there was nothing I could do about it.

෮෮෮

What does the Bible say about hope? Proverbs 13:12 reads, "Delayed hope makes the heart sick, but fulfilled desire is a tree of life." The young girl that I was had one terribly sick heart. I had lost hope in ever getting what I needed from my parents. Loss, however you experience it, leaves a mark on your soul. I lost my mother every other weekend on the ride home from her house.

For a long time, there was just the smallest amount of hope that maybe this time I would get to stay with her and everything would be better. Then I would ride home and all hope would be lost again. Week after week, month after month, hope faded to something I remembered, not something I felt.

For so many years, even as an adult in a healthy and happy marriage, I couldn't listen to 70s music. The melodies actually made me feel ill. I felt badly for my husband because he loves 70s tunes. For him, they always brought back happy memories of the love and security he was surrounded with as a child. With me, however, whenever one of those familiar tunes would come on the radio, he would quickly change the station because it would remind him I wasn't as fortunate as he had been. And, of course being the wonderful man he is, he wanted to protect me from any sadness.

I had always attributed my dislike for the music to the sexual abuse I had suffered. But as I have asked the Lord to help me understand myself so that I can release all of the places in me in need of healing, He has shown me it was the loss I felt on those car rides home that gave the music the power to make my heart sick. The music was one of my replay buttons.

Up until a few years ago, even being in the same room with my mom caused an ache in me. I missed her, yet she was sitting right there. I realized the little girl that I had been was still missing the mommy I had always hoped to have. The aching sadness came because that time was lost, and I could never get it back. She hadn't been what I had needed her to be, and she never would be. The opportunity was lost, and even if we could magically go back and have the time to do over, she would not be able to do much better: For whatever reason, my mom just doesn't have it in her.

It's interesting how abuse and loss can affect a person throughout her life. I met my husband when I was 21. We had been dating for about a month when I asked him if he would come see my mom with me. I thought I had located her but was nervous to go by myself.

I had decided a year before that I would not call her until she called me. I still desperately wanted her to reach out and show me love. After a year of no calls, however, I decided my stupid game didn't prove anything, and I needed to find her. I needed to make sure she was okay.

I discovered that she was living in an apartment with her boyfriend in a city south of where I lived. Once again, even as an adult, I was dying inside to be loved by someone who was supposed to love me back the way I wanted to be loved.

☙☙☙

As I was praying about writing this particular chapter, I asked the Lord for help. (Always a good idea, I have found.) So I asked the Lord, "What does Your Word say about loss?" The Holy Spirit encouraged me to read the book of Job. I already knew what the book was about and had even read bits and pieces of it. But, let's face it, except for the last few paragraphs, it's kind of depressing. God allows Job to be put through the ringer by Satan. Job's worldly possessions are stripped from him, his children killed, he is covered from head to toe in painful boils and his wife basically attacks his manhood because he refuses to curse God and die.

If you want to feel better about the depth of your own garbage, spend some time reading about Job. That should lift your spirits. Occasionally, while I was reading this chapter, I would jump forward to the end just to remind myself it was going to get better. One of the things that had bothered me most about the book was it almost seemed as though God was playing a game with Job. Lucifer came to God and challenged God to a game at Job's expense. This reminded me of my childhood and my feelings about the Lord. Was my life just a game to God? Did all of these horrible things happen to me just for someone or lots of someone's sick pleasure?

What spoke to me the most in the book of Job was actually the last few paragraphs. This was a bit of a surprise since I had always thought of the ending as the good part, where everything turns out great and everyone is happy.

As I got to the end this time, it felt more like a cliffhanger than a happy ending to a tragic story. There was more to understand in the ending than I had comprehended before. God restores Job and blesses him more in the latter than in the former part of his life.

But what about his 10 children who had died? Yes, the Lord blessed Job with 10 more children, even more beautiful than the previous batch. But I know if I were Job, this new blessing would not make up for the 10 lost to me! I have no doubt Job loved those 10 children that were dead as much as I love my own children. So I found myself wondering how Job felt about the loss of what could not be replaced. Unfortunately, the book ended without an answer to my question.

So here is what I have learned: Sometimes we don't get to understand why God allows heartache and pain. The book of Job tells us even the most innocent, undeserving people will suffer great tragedy and loss, while God is still to be seen as loving, compassionate and correct. The bottom line is: God is God, and we are not. He is sovereign. God's purpose and glory is unchanging, even when evil and pain are permitted. His ways are not our ways (Isaiah 55:8, Job 11:7-9).

We are refined by the fire (1 Peter 1:6-8). Those last few paragraphs of Job don't hold the secret recipe to how to have peace in circumstances that seem impossible to recover from. I can't give anyone a roadmap of how it came to be that I can listen to 70s music and enjoy it with my husband now or how the aching in my heart and soul for my lost childhood is gone. But it is gone.

As trite as it may seem, the only answer I can give is that the truth has set me free. Since that time I spent on the chapel floor, allowing the Lord to wrench my heart open to Him and expose every ugly lie I believed, He has replaced the ache with a peace I didn't know was possible.

I realized Job's healing wasn't in the restoration of or the replacing of what he lost. I think most of us look at Job's wife and think about how awful she was for how she treated Job, demanding he curse God. Perhaps we should look at the two of them and their individual reactions to tragedy. She must have had immeasurable grief and anger at the loss of her children. Is it so unthinkable that she may have gone through a period of hating God for what had happened to her life? She looked at God as the problem instead of the answer. Job was able to bear the burden of loss because he found strength to go on in the Lord. God loved Job and comforted him in a way only He can, and Job received that love and healing. Because Job received God's healing, he was able to find joy in God's blessing, his new family and restored life.

The difference between "before the chapel floor" and now is the truth isn't just words on a page for me anymore. Now it is what I believe. The truth is what I know in my heart, not just in my head.

My 12-year-old daughter, Trinity, won't go to the car at night to retrieve her backpack she forgot to bring in after school. Someone has to go with her because it's dark out, and she's scared.

"Scared of what?" we ask. "There is nothing out there, and the car is right near the house." Rick and I can sit and talk to Trinity about the fact there is absolutely nothing out there that will harm her, and she will agree, but she still won't go get the backpack without someone.

There is a big difference between believing what the truth is and knowing the truth. To know truth, we have to actually walk in it and live it out. This is one of the reasons Paul said in Philippians 2:12-13, "Work out your own salvation with fear and trembling. For it is God working in you, [enabling you] both to will and to act for His good purpose."

This doesn't mean we are to ask for salvation every day. It means we are to walk daily in Christ with new revelations of who He is (truth) and who He has created us to be.

So how do we get to living the truth, as well as knowing the truth? The Bible says we will be "transformed by the renewing of our minds" (Romans 12:2). After my week at camp, I began to devour the gospels of the Bible. I wanted to hear the story of Jesus from every angle. I wanted to replace any false belief I had with the truth of His Word. I needed to clean out my mind and allow the Lord to renew my thoughts and beliefs and bring them into alignment with His thoughts and truths.

LAYING IT DOWN

"White as snow." As I kneel here on the floor, I'm beginning to understand what the term "white as snow" means. How many hymns and worship songs have we heard with those words? As a single snowflake falls to the earth, it is clean and pure. It sparkles as the light reflects off its many prism-like surfaces. It has not yet been tainted by whatever ground it will land on. As it slowly dances its way to the earth, it is perfect in its uniqueness. It is fresh and clean and beautifully untouched. When a few million are grouped together and blanket the landscape, it appears to be the whitest white you will ever see on God's canvas.

I am starting to see the many times God knocked at the door to my heart, and I turned away from His pursuit because I didn't know who He really was. I could not bear for Him or anyone else to see the shame I hid deep inside myself. I couldn't even stand to see or acknowledge it myself, so I would pretend it wasn't there. Like small children who hide in plain sight: They believe if they cover their face and shut their eyes tightly, you can't see them because they can't see you.

I cannot ignore God anymore. I'm tired of running and hiding and pretending like I'm something or someone I am not. I want everything He has for me. The Holy Spirit has been giving me glimpses of the freedom that is my right as a child of God, and now I cannot go back. I want "white as snow." "Throw me in a snow bank, Lord!"

I want to feel as clean as a new, shimmering, untouched snowflake on its fluttering journey to the earth. I feel like I am being bathed in my own tears. The layers of shame I've carried on me like tarnish on silver are being scrubbed away.

It's about the fifth day of camp, and we are almost to the end. I know the Lord isn't done with me yet. I tell my husband I'm ready to go talk to Pastor Daren. Rick has been talking to him all along and encouraging me to go and share with him what is happening, but up until this point, I felt like that would be intrusive on what the pastor is here to accomplish. Part of me was still looking for a way out, saying it's not about me but about the teens who are paying to attend this camp. But now I'm becoming greedy to find that clean place where the dirty residue covering me will be washed away forever.

As I have soaked in the Lord's presence on the floor amidst all these other young troubled and hurting souls, I am realizing that I am not just grieving for what was stolen from me, but also for the damage I freely inflicted upon myself. I know I have to keep moving forward on the journey the Lord has set me upon. But this new revelation brings new fears: I am afraid to face not only what was done to me, but what I did to myself.

చిలిచిలి

At 12 years old, I felt like I finally had some control over some things in my life. My sister's behavior got worse and worse, and since she was making my stepmom's life a nightmare, the ever-present family counselor suggested to my dad that he should just let her go live with our mom. I think the whole family was getting weary of the constant battles for power between my sister and my parents. And, of course, because it was suggested by the family counselor, it must be done.

There really wasn't much talk about me going, too. It was a strange thing. Here was what I had been living for as long as I could remember: a chance to finally be with my mom. I could have thrown a fit and protested that I should be allowed to go as well. I could have made my case to the counselor who had the final say in all things. But I didn't. Things had changed for me so much that when my sister left, I stayed where I was.

The major change in my life was that I had finally developed friendships. I liked my school. For me, this was the longest I had ever been in one place, attending the same school district. I felt connected to something, and I wasn't willing to give that up.

More importantly, I had a boyfriend, and he was the center of my world. In my mind there was no rhyme or reason as to why he liked me. He was popular, good-looking, on the football team, from the nicer side of town and on and on.

I, on the other hand, was sometimes mistaken for a boy, skinny enough to be called gangly and dealing with a constant battle against pubescent acne. From the shock on my friends' faces when the news started to circulate about him and me, I was pretty certain my assessment of myself was accurate.

My boyfriend was nearly two years older than I (another plus in my book of "what makes a cool boyfriend"), and everyone knew who he was. I would have done anything to make him happy, and if it meant staying in my unhappy home to be near him, I would do it. So when my sister left to live with our mother, I didn't make a stink about not going with her.

For a while, life was bliss with my new boyfriend, my new popularity and my new privacy in a bedroom all by myself. I had stuffed all that fear and anxiety garbage somewhere deep inside myself where I kept it locked in remission most of the time. I lived for the time I would leave my embarrassing house and be the happy, lucky girl other girls envied. My boyfriend told me often of his love for me, and we conspired to spend as much time together as possible. If our parents said no, we would find ways to be together behind their backs. I felt mildly guilty about this, but the way I felt when my boyfriend looked at me with what I believed was love in his eyes, and my friends with envy in theirs, outweighed any guilt.

My friends became less and less important to me as he became more and more important. On my 13th birthday, my boyfriend bought me a nice gift. I think it was a baseball tee with the words "I love blank" on it (the blank being his name). No boy had ever bought me a gift before, so I wore that shirt proudly, like a banner across my chest!

On the other hand, when his birthday came a few

months later, I had no way to get him anything. So I gave him the only thing I could think of. It was really what he wanted more than anything else from me. I knew this because he had told me often, "If we really loved each other," we would do "IT." I knew what he meant — "The Big IT."

I gave him what was left of my virginity as a birthday gift. I told myself, *This time I decided.* I thought, *He's not taking it without my consent; I gave it freely.* I told myself this so it would seem completely different than before. I told myself I was in control this time, so there was nothing to be sad or disappointed about. That's what I told myself over and over.

Any feelings of shame or dirtiness trying to creep up on me I just shoved into the place I kept especially for those sorts of feelings. So what if I had wanted to save that pure piece of myself for marriage? I was a women in control now, so I got to do what I wanted, and what I wanted was for my boyfriend to love me and know how important he was to me.

Our relationship went on from there, with the physical part of it continuing as well. I didn't particularly like the physical part, but I was willing to continue because it was just part of being in a "mature" and "significant" relationship. I just had to work a little harder to keep the dirty feelings tucked away where they couldn't hurt me so much.

Since I was just barely 13 years old and had only recently started having menstrual periods, they weren't quite regular yet. In fact, I think I had only had two or three, and they had been months apart. So when I didn't have one for a while I didn't really think much of it. I didn't realize I was pregnant until I actually started having symptoms. I began to be exhausted all the time, had sudden cravings for strange things like bologna and hot sauce and, of course, the voluptuous changes occurred in my normally lanky body.

When I finally realized I wasn't just having a growth spurt, I was terrified. I didn't want to have a baby. There were things I wanted to accomplish, like finishing junior high! I was so disappointed in myself. My boyfriend, however, was actually excited about the prospect of parenthood. He started making plans for our future together.

I was sick as I felt my world closing in around me. This was not what I wanted! I was doing this to be in charge! Those ugly, familiar feelings of being out of control and trapped in despair were creeping up on me again, and I couldn't seem to shove them down. This time, it was my fault. I had done this dirty stupid thing to me.

After another month of pretending my condition was something other than pregnancy and trying to find the perfect way to tell my dad and stepmom about my predicament, I finally got up the nerve and just spilled it. Having breast milk leak through my shirt while I dozed on my desk in math class brought the depth of my situation into a more realistic perspective for me.

Dad took my news stoically at first. He drove me to a

clinic and had me have a pregnancy test. The nurse I talked to alone took one look at the protruding hard belly hidden under my loose shirt and told me a test was hardly necessary since the proof was in front of me. Regardless, we did the test, and it was positive. She said I was probably around four and a half to five months along. I walked out to the waiting room and told my dad the news … again. He quietly got up and walked to the car with his wife and me trailing behind.

When we got back to the house, I settled into the far corner of the couch with my knees drawn up to my chest like a shield against what I knew was coming. He asked me what the test result had been. So, again, I told him I was pregnant. And then he lost it.

My dad was beyond angry. He roared at me, screaming that I was to have an abortion, and that was going to be the end of it. Then he looked right over to his wife and grumbled, "I say she gets an abortion. What do you say?"

Wow, Dad! I thought, *what happened to being Catholic?* Hidden behind my knees, I told him in quiet defiance he couldn't make me.

I wish I could say I never contemplated killing my baby, but the truth is I knew I was too far along, and it wasn't an option anymore. My father leaned over me and raised his hand like he was going to punch me. The fist hovered there for what seemed like forever, while he decided what he was going to do with it. During that eternity, so many things went through my head that I wanted to spit out at him. Like blaming him for what I had been doing. I wanted to throw back in his face how he had "taught" me what I was supposed to do with my boyfriends. While I held my tongue, he thought better of landing a punch I knew he wanted to throw so badly and stalked out.

After the initial blow up, my dad didn't talk to me about my pregnancy again. In fact, he completely ignored me after that and only spoke to me if it was absolutely necessary. My boyfriend was banned from my life, and I wasn't allowed to go anywhere except school.

While my boyfriend was busy sneaking me large bottles of orange juice and healthy snacks into a designated bush outside my house, I started making plans. My mom was aware of my situation and the fact that my dad hadn't even taken me to a doctor yet, other than for the pregnancy test. After a few months of planning and secretly taking my belongings to school, then dropping them off at a friend's house to be picked up later by my mom, I ran away to live with her permanently. As easy as that, I moved in with my mom, along with her current husband and my sister.

My mom and I went to the courthouse to see what we had to do for her to take back custody for medical coverage purposes. Turned out my dad never actually filed those cursed custody papers he had loved waving in my face. Yes, he had filled them out, but he had never gotten around to filing them legally. It literally took 30 minutes at the courthouse to gain that significant piece of information! My mom had had custody of us all along. At that time, I didn't dwell on the fact she hadn't taken the time to find out sooner. I had bigger issues at that moment, and I needed her too much. I thought, *This time, she had to come through for me! Right?*

My mom got me to a doctor shortly after that. At my first appointment, I was six and a half months pregnant, and my baby was growing at a healthy rate. I was happy to be with my mom and sister again, but was sad to be so far from my baby's father. My mom lived an hour away from him, so we were only able to see each other on weekends. On the outside I tried to stay positive and take my life one day at a time. I tried not to contemplate the future too much because when I did, the anxiousness would swell like a balloon nearing the bursting point.

I held my head up and tried to ignore the looks I got from strangers as my belly grew beyond my ability to hide it under baggy clothes. I was not one of those 13 year olds that looked 18 or 19. Heck, I'm not sure I looked 13. But I definitely wasn't mistaken for a boy anymore!

I tried to focus on the baby growing inside me. What would it look like? I looked forward to having someone to love that would love me in return. I had put my baby dolls away only two years before, so I imagined playing with my baby the way I had played with my dolls. I was somehow certain she was a girl, so I imagined dressing her up in frilly dresses and pretty shoes. Always I focused on keeping myself distracted so the feelings of fear, dread and guilt would stay below the surface, and I could function.

࿇࿇࿇

If there is one thing I learned from my time in that camp chapel, it is that *healing is a process.* There are many steps to take on the journey toward wholeness. One of the steps I had to take was forgiving myself ... and forgiving myself ... and forgiving myself.

Because of the price Jesus paid on the cross for us, we can ask for and receive forgiveness from God for our transgressions. But often, instead of receiving what is freely given, we hold on to the guilt and shame attached to the sin. As I stated above in regard to forgiving my earthly father, hate is an emotion that is easy to control. By this I mean we can mold it into something we believe we control. But love, on the other hand, is difficult. Love takes action, trust and time. I had to learn to forgive myself, which meant I had to recognize that I actually hated parts of me. From there I had to learn to love myself. To believe that I was a "new creation" and, by grace, worthy of being loved.

Guilt is just another tool used by the enemy to keep us quiet. When you're feeling like a loser and a fraud all the time, you are certainly not going to be out spreading the good news of Jesus. The enemy's tactics are to produce permanent thought processes that produce certain outcomes. When the tape recorder in our head starts playing, "I'm not a good person. God could not love someone like me. I am not worthy of anyone's love," etc. ... forgiving yourself, like forgiving others, can be a daily ritual. Sometimes it can even feel like an every-second-of-the-day exercise.

Every time guilt rears its ugly head, we have to bring it to the Lord and say, "Lord, I give this to You. I receive Your love and forgiveness." Every time we do this, every time we play God's tape of His promises instead of the one the enemy has conditioned us with, the bondage that guilt and shame keeps us in loosens its grip. When you begin to replace those thoughts with the truths from God's Word, those other thoughts begin to get crowded out (or straightened out).

Over time, as the outcomes the enemy wants are not produced because we continually choose to go straight to God and tell Him we receive what He is freely giving us, the enemy loses his stranglehold on our body, mind and spirit. As I wrote earlier, this is not the power of positive thinking. It is the power of God's promises brought about in our lives by the grace of Christ's work on the cross. God's Word is living! It is Christ in the flesh. John 1:1-5 reads, "In the beginning was the Word, and the Word was with God, and the Word was God. He was with God in the beginning. All things were created through Him, and apart from Him not one thing was created that has been created. Life was in Him, and that life was the light of men. That light shines in the darkness, yet the darkness did not overcome it."

His Word has the power because it is alive, power to bring light into my darkness. It will not be overcome by the darkness of my past! And His Word has the power to bring life! I must bring His living Word to the depths of my being so I can be transformed by it. Hebrews 4:12 reads, "For the Word of God is living and effective and sharper than any two-edged sword, penetrating as far as to divide soul, spirit, joints and marrow; it is a judge of the ideas and thoughts of the heart." I needed the lies cut away and replaced with the truth of who I was created to be in Christ.

Romans 8:1 reads, "Therefore, no condemnation now exists for those in Christ Jesus, because the Spirit's law of life in Christ Jesus has set you free from the law of sin and death." The word "condemn" means to be guilty. This verse is promising us that the guilt for your sin and mine is gone under what Jesus accomplished on the cross. When I said the sinner's prayer and received Jesus as my Lord and Savior, He took all my sin, and because of what He did, I am now justified. I am a new creation and a daughter of the King.

I would encourage anyone to read all of Romans 8 and declare the truth found there in his or her own life. I am not who I used to be, and I will not choose to put on the old coat of my former self. Instead, I will put on the coat of my true identity in Christ. Sometimes, when I start to feel myself slipping back into my old train of thought or I hear the now faint background noise of that old tape, I will picture myself taking an old dirty coat off and putting a beautiful new coat on.

When I was thinking and praying about Biblical examples for the issue of guilt, King David kept coming to mind. The Lord was with David, but He wasn't always pleased with David. Second Samuel, chapters 11 and 12, tell the story of how David committed adultery with Uriah's wife, Bathsheba, and after he was informed she had conceived, David then sent Uriah to the frontlines of war to ensure the man would die in battle. David wanted the man's wife for himself, even though she was Uriah's only wife. David already had many wives and concubines. As King, he had his choice of women, but David coveted what he could not rightfully have. And so Uriah died in battle, and David married his widow. The Lord had blessed David in so many ways and would have continued to bless David even more, but David got greedy and selfish. In committing murder, he sinned against God by doing what the Lord considered evil.

God sent Nathan, a prophet in the royal court, to tell David how disgusted He was with David's evildoings. David repents, and Nathan tells him the Lord has taken away his sin; he will not die. But because of the contempt David showed for the Lord in his sin, David's son born to Bathsheba would die. The baby becomes ill and is sick for seven days, dying on the seventh day.

During those seven days, David fasted and prayed and wept for the child, refusing to be comforted. He didn't bathe or eat or do anything other than lay on the floor and cry out to the Lord to change His mind. But on the seventh day, when David finds out the child is dead, he gets up, washes himself, dresses in clean clothes and eats. When the servants are perplexed at his behavior, David says to them, "While the baby was alive, I fasted and wept because I thought, 'Who knows? The Lord may be gracious to me and let him live.' But now that he is dead, why should I fast? Can I bring him back again? I'll go to him, but he will never return to me."

David is a favorite Bible character of mine because he is blatantly imperfect with moments of greatness, thanks to God's hand in his life. When he has his eye on the Lord, he accomplishes great things. What I liked about this story is King David knew when to let his guilt go. Once it was clear he could do nothing to change the outcome, he got up from his weeping and moved forward.

When I was focusing so much of my energy on feeling guilty about the mess I had made of the mess I came from, my focus wasn't on God. It was on me. The child I continued to mourn was me. Much like David, I needed to recognize that I was not going to get a "do-over."

I'm not talking about the wooing of the Holy Spirit that can gently guide us to the Lord and to asking for forgiveness as we should. I am speaking of the guilt we continually pick back up after we have brought our sin to the Lord and carry around like emotional saddlebags. It is an unnecessary burden the Lord has not asked us to carry.

We certainly wouldn't strap 20-pound weights to our shoulders and lug them around everywhere we go like they belonged there. But what we are not willing to do in the physical realm, we are more than willing to do in the spiritual. The choice to give up the burden of guilt is our choice to make.

PERFECTING THE MASK

There are a few new grownup faces this year at camp. Some returning familiar faces as well. One particular woman has been a presence in my life for many years; having her here this week has given me a peace she probably is completely unaware of. It isn't exactly that we're close. She is just someone I know I can trust, and she has been present and available to pray for me when I needed someone. She is a very small woman with a very powerful presence, and I'm so glad she's here this week.

The new faces belong to two women who have just recently begun to work with our youth group. They're both a bit older than me in years, but a youthful vitality emanates from them, and I am certain they are a good fit for our youth group. I love how they work together as a team, and I am even a little jealous because I don't have a female friend I'm that close with anymore.

I am comforted knowing these women are here this week. All three have a wisdom about them that has come from years of being with and hearing from the Lord.

My husband and I catch up to Daren walking from the cafeteria to our rooms. It's about a five-minute walk, so there is just enough time to start the difficult conversation I want to have with him. It's hard to even know where to begin. I know I want something to change, something to be fixed, but I have to admit even before I open my mouth, I'm starting to lose hope that anything will be a long-term fix. I'm thinking about all the Christian self-help books I have started and put down because I jumped forward after becoming impatient, hoping for an answer, only to be disappointed. There was definitely a spiritual battle going on.

I was gaining the strength to desire a change, but once I left the chapel floor, the floodgate of emotions and fear (lies from the enemy) would get unbearably loud. All I know is I'm lonely and angry in the deepest part of me, and I want to feel better. As I wrote earlier, I can be in a room full of people I love and who love me and still feel lonely.

I tell the pastor, "I think I need to be healed from my past." Yep, that's what I need. Like I said, at this point, I'm not very hopeful. Even though I'm embarrassed about what I've done and what I've been through, I can talk to people about it in a very "nonchalant" way. So I tell my pastor friend a little about myself, like it's no big deal for me to talk about it, and he tells me he would like to spend some time praying with me after the service that night. He says it would probably be best if I had a female I trust there while we pray, and I know just who to ask.

∿∿∿

It was nearly time for my daughter to be born. I felt like my body was already stretched to its limits. At each visit, the doctor would tell me, "This is when the baby is gaining all its baby fat." I was pretty certain my little body couldn't accommodate any more growth from the mammoth-sized fetus inside me. Each week I would go back, and each week he would tell me everything was looking good. Oh, and other kind, self-esteem-building comments like, "Well, your breasts are starting to look like erupting volcanoes." He let me know in subtle and not so subtle ways that he did not approve of me. I wasn't very fond of him, either. I couldn't sleep comfortably for more than a few hours at a time, and I was dying to see this kid hidden inside me.

Two weeks after my due date, when I was beginning to think the baby had taken up permanent residence atop my pea-sized bladder, I woke in the middle of the night to a serious cramp that had me holding my breath until it ended. I woke my mom and told her this time it hurt for real, not like all the pretend contractions we had spent hours counting in front of the television at night. To my immense relief, the contractions didn't stop when I got up to get my stuff and walk out to the car. If anything, they got worse.

I was ecstatic! It was finally happening. The excitement lasted about another hour at the hospital, and then reality set in. It hurt so much, I kept thinking, *It can't get worse*, and then it did. The pain was more than anything I could have imagined. I was stoic on the outside but frantic on the inside. *Please help me, please help me,* was the repeating chant running through my head.

After what seemed like a million years, the doctor decided I was progressing enough to have a spinal, and just like that, all the pain was gone. Funny thing those spinals — at one point my leg actually fell off the bed, and I didn't realize it. I told my boyfriend it felt like something was pulling at my back and side, and when he investigated, he found my leg dangling from the side of the bed. If that weren't embarrassing enough, there was a mysterious popping sound followed by a foul odor. That was pretty much the end of any dignity I might have had left.

It was another six hours before I got to meet my daughter Tiffany for the first time. It was the strangest thing when they handed her to me in her first moments. The anticipation had been so overwhelming that for just a second or two I couldn't turn my head to look at her. I'm sure nobody else noticed my hesitation, but I remember it like every millisecond was stretched out into an hour. She was a cute little wide-eyed thing with her squished pink face. After a minute or two of us learning each other's faces, she was whisked away to be bathed and measured.

Once she was gone, I had a chance to look around the room at the hospital staff that had helped my body go through the birthing process. When I looked into their half-covered faces, their eyes told me they were mad at me and disappointed. There weren't the usual congratulations and smiles giving encouragement to the new mother. Instead there were just stern looks and silent glances in my direction. Nobody was happy to be sending a defenseless infant home with a 14-year-old child.

I was suddenly overwhelmingly tired. I wanted to

escape the sterile room and my life. So I willingly gave into the exhaustion that went all the way to my soul.

I don't know how long I slept, but when I woke up, I was in a dark room with a woman washing me with warm soapy water. I was still so tired it was hard to really wake all the way up. She washed me like I was a fragile piece of glass she was trying not to break.

I remember her saying nice things to me in a comforting way. I was happily relieved she wasn't mad at me. I don't know how I came to that conclusion, but I knew this woman saw me for what I really was: a terrified, hurting little girl who had just been through one of the most traumatic experiences a woman can go through. I don't think I ever met her while I was awake, but of all the people I encountered at the hospital, the memory of her kindness will stay with me always.

Both my mom and Tiffany's father's family were overjoyed to see her and hold her. I felt somewhat detached, like I was watching it all from a distance. I would make the appropriate responses and smile for the pictures, but I was neither happy nor sad. I felt like I was a hundred years old. I was weary in a way I didn't know a body could be. I was relieved when it was time for everyone to leave, and I could go home with my baby and my mom.

I was better at home. I felt confident in my ability to take care of Tiffany. I was up when she was up, and I slept when she slept. Although my body was sore, it at least felt like my body again. My first night home, my mom made me spaghetti, and I ate a whole plate full. I was amazed at how much I had missed being able to fit more than a couple spoonfuls of food in me.

On the second night home, I had just finished sitting in a shallow bath to ease some of the discomfort of the stitches when everything fell apart. After my bath, I sat on the couch with a large bed pillow under me, and my mom handed my daughter to me. I felt a warm dampness between my legs, and at first I thought it was the bath water. As I handed Tiffany to my sister, I looked down at my lap and saw the blood turning my light blue robe crimson.

I was shocked and terrified. I knew I was dying. The blood was running out of me like a faucet had been turned on. My mom was on the phone to the doctor, and he said she should massage my stomach to make it slow down and that this was normal. I knew this was definitely not normal. As she massaged, I could feel the flow slow down and eventually stop. The whole incident was about five minutes long. After that, the rest of the night was a blur.

My mom must have gotten me cleaned up and into bed. Every so often I remember she would check on me and rub my stomach some more. I didn't get up for anything other than trips to the bathroom because I was terrified to move. I didn't roll over or move in any way, except to readjust my ankles, either crossed with the left foot on top or crossed with the right foot on top, like I was somehow going to protect myself from bleeding to death in that position.

I began to rub my own stomach when Mom decided I was out of danger and no longer came in to rub it herself. Over the next few days that became my routine. Crossing and re-crossing my legs so tightly that my ankles were bruised and rubbing my stomach almost constantly while I was awake, causing my lower abdomen to be bruised and tender. In my unreasonable fear, I decided the pain was better than dying.

The fear was back, and it was all-consuming. I thought of nothing but seeing my blood pouring out of me and killing me painlessly. This made me terribly afraid to sleep.

Over the next few weeks, my body started to heal. My nail beds and lips turned pink again, and I could get out of bed to take care of my daughter. Eventually, my brain started to believe I wasn't in imminent danger of bleeding to death, but the fear stuck. I couldn't seem to shake it. The fear was fiercer than when I was younger.

For the last couple of years, I had been able to keep it mostly at bay, locked away like it wasn't really mine. Now I began to have night terrors again and a belief that I was going crazy. Nothing but daylight made me feel better, and that only lasted so long. I was desperate to feel safe and secure, but this time not even being near my mom helped. Eventually, the fear followed me into the daytime.

It was like a floodgate had been opened, and I could not get it back into the locked position. Everything had changed, and there was never going to be any going back to life before all this. Nothing about my life was ever going to feel like freedom again. Granted, the brief freedom I had between the ages of about 11 and 13 wasn't great, but anyone who has suffered from long-term fear and anxiety will take whatever break she can get. The night I hemorrhaged, my poor choices almost took my life. As the weeks and months passed, I began to see how my choices had taken my life, at least the life I was used to and the life I hoped to make for myself. It was never going to be just mine alone again. From now on it was "our" life, Tiffany's and mine.

I needed to get things back under control like I had had them before. I needed to get all this craziness locked back away where I could control its effect on me. I was determined to feel on the inside the way I showed myself on the outside. I tried to never let anyone know what was happening on the inside, how consumed I was with unexplainable dread. I was convinced if people actually knew what was going on inside me, they would know I was crazy. I had great fear of what they would think of me.

I didn't share with anyone how I was feeling because it was just too scary to put into words. I didn't want to make it as real as that, so I pretended I wasn't living daily in the prisons that were my thoughts. Friends or family would comment on my ability to handle so much so well at such a young age, and I would smile and say, "You do what you have to." On the inside, a little girl was screaming at the top of her lungs, "HELP ME!"

❧❧❧

Isaiah 41:10 reads, "Do not fear, for I am with you; do not be afraid, for I am your God. I will strengthen you; I will help you; I will hold on to you with My righteous right hand." Oh, to know then what I know now. Back then, I was searching for strength in myself because I did not know there was someone else I could rely on for strength. My life until then had only shown me how those I should have been able to count on were always more likely to let me down or hurt me even more.

So over the years I had developed the belief that I had to be my own rock, my own steadfast ground to stand on. On the chapel floor, surrounded by people who loved me, God wanted to show me I did not need to rely on my own strength. The floor I had created to stand on was more like glass than rock, and the burdens of my past were stacked up precariously, like stones on a pallet sitting atop my shoulders.

Unfortunately, in the stooped position I stand in to balance the burden, my eyes are always on the ground. I don't chance moving forward and possibly disturbing a stone that could ultimately shatter the ground I stand on. I also can't look around me to see who might be beside me to lend a hand.

This time, Jesus was telling me He would carry the burden for me, so I could look around and see the help He had brought into my life. When I looked around, I saw Rick, this wonderfully loving man, who would take on the world for me if I needed him to, and some very strong, wise women, who were willing to stand in the gap for me.

It was no accident or coincidence that those three special women were at camp with me.

WILL THE REAL JESUS PLEASE STAND UP

When you were a kid, did you ever throw a Popsicle stick into a stream and follow it on its bumpy path downstream? I have. The stick gets bounced around in the current, occasionally getting stuck in some hidden place, until the current grabs hold of it and carries it back into sight. The rushing water then sweeps it away to carry it farther downstream. Though the Popsicle stick was hidden from my sight from time to time on its journey, I would catch a glimpse of it and eagerly follow to see where it eventually would land.

I see that Popsicle stick as the seed of my faith and the stream's current as the Lord in my life.

At some point in mine and Tiffany's relationship with her dad's family, they took me to a Billy Graham Crusade being held in the Tacoma Dome. It was an amazing production with the booming worship hymns and huge crowds of people raising their hands to the Lord. It was a far cry from the Catholic "stand up, sit down, peace to your neighbor" dance of my dad's church. Pastor Billy Graham himself was such a presence up there on stage, he had my undivided attention, and when he called for the sinners to repent and give their hearts to the Lord, I timidly made my way to the floor in front of the stage.

At the Billy Graham crusade I gave my heart to the Lord and affirmed my faith that there was a God who was real. As I've written, I always seemed to have a sense that there was a God, and I knew somehow, some way, I needed to be saved. I believe the truth of what was preached that night fell on good soil and took deep root. But my faith in God got bounced around a lot at times. His Holy Spirit was the current that would pull me back to the path He had for me. There were times when the stream became more like a raging river, and the small Popsicle stick that was my faith got thrown here and there. Sometimes it seemed so far from me as to be forgotten, but the Lord has always been faithful to grab hold of me and pull me back to the current that leads to Him. I didn't come to an understanding of what it meant to be saved from myself and the world by actually making Jesus the Lord of my life, however, until I was 21. (More about that later.)

As camp was wrapping up and we were heading to our last evening session, I was reminded of the bumpy ride that had brought me to this point. I was determined to keep moving toward what God had for me. I wanted to give control to Him so I could finally rest.

꒰꒱꒰

After many months of struggling for control of the fear and anxiety that threatened to destroy me, I got myself back in order. I shoved all the garbage back into its appointed place inside of me and worked to avoid any triggers that might bring up anything unpleasant. Back to the stream metaphor, my life and feelings were like a raging river that I had forced into a man-made channel that was controlled by dikes and a dam. One small break in the dike or a release of too much emotion from the dam and I knew the river would be raging. I took great pride in my ability to overcome my circumstances and control that river.

As soon as school started at the alternative high school I now attended, I threw myself into being the best student I could. I was determined to finish school, while raising my daughter at the same time. Tiffany was able to come to school with me every day and spend the day in the daycare, while I went to classes. My elective classes were spent in a mandatory parenting class and nursery. I welcomed the normalcy of attending school with other teenagers. It made it easier to pretend I was just like all of them.

Of course, I wasn't normal at all. I was a 14-year-old mother engaged to my daughter's 16-year-old father. He and his dad were converting a garage on some property into a house we would live in. Everything was planned out for me.

My boyfriend was adamant that I be home every evening at 7 so he could call and make sure everything was okay. He would get very angry and hurt if I ever made plans that interfered with that nightly phone call. At school I was trying to appear happy and put together, while in reality, I was so stressed out I felt one small tear in my façade and I would blow apart into a million pieces.

One day, when my daughter was about a year old, I got up the courage to end it with her dad. The great and passionate love I had thought I had for him had turned into loathing of the stranglehold I felt he had on my life.

As I walked away from him that day, I literally felt like I was walking on air. I wasn't happy about hurting him because he was Tiffany's dad. I was just so elated to feel the freedom again. *Now,* I thought, *I can make my own choices without being manipulated by someone else's desires.*

Tiffany's dad was very hurt and angry at first. But after some initial retaliation, we settled into a routine of every other weekend visitations for Tiffany, and life went on.

On my free weekends, I started hanging out more with friends, and I felt like things were pretty good and steady. I had also started speaking on "teen parent panels" at different high schools in the area. My parenting teacher had started the panels to show other teenagers, hopefully, the reality of being a teen parent. I felt I was doing something good in helping to prevent more teen pregnancies. All in all, I decided things were going very well.

In the time I had come to live with my mom and sister, my mom had divorced again. Her husband had gone out of the country for a job, and I guess they decided a long-distance relationship wasn't going to work for them. That husband had a serious problem with alcohol, but he wasn't unkind or scary to me, so I was a little sad to see him go. But not at all surprised.

While things seemed to be steady with school and home, I was unaware that my mom had started dating someone new pretty seriously. I guess I was so focused on myself, I missed what was happening around me.

My mom came home from work one day and asked to have a talk with my sister and me. She told us she had met someone, and they were married now. THEY WERE MARRIED NOW! My mom and her next husband were moving into their own place.

And just like that, my world turned upside down again. My sister and I were 15 and 16 years old, with a baby!

Not again, Mom, I thought. *How can you do this to us again?* She told us not to worry because she wasn't going to let the apartment complex know that she had left, so we should be able to stay as long as we wished. My sister had a part-time job at a taco joint, and I had $300 a month in welfare. We weren't going to be able to cover the rent, and she knew it. When I pointed that out to her, she said maybe we could get a roommate. I wanted to scream at her, *ALL OF MY FRIENDS LIVE WITH THEIR PARENTS, MOM!* The anger inside of me was deafening. *THIS CAN'T BE HAPPENING!* But it was happening … and within a few days, she was gone.

৵৵৵

I'm sorry, did I say that Popsicle stick got "bounced" around? It would be more accurate to say SLAMMED against jagged rocks and occasionally forced under the water until jerked loose! I guess it is easy to understand why I have some trust issues that have followed me into my Christian life. I wanted very badly to believe all the beautiful scriptures about a loving, trustworthy God who is faithful to have your back in times of trial, but my experience with people gave me an altered perspective of Him. You know the scripture in Luke 11 that reads, "What father among you, if his son asks for a fish, would give him a snake instead of a fish? Or if he asks for an egg, will give him a scorpion? If you then, who are evil know how to give good gifts to your children, how much more will your Heavenly Father give the Holy Spirit to those who ask Him?" Yeah, I would have been happy to have one of those evil good gift givers.

Well, the good news is He is not "people"; He is God. He has your back, front and both sides! We are created in His image, not the other way around. People live in a fallen world. People have a corrupted nature, and people will always disappoint, whether they mean to or not. As my week at camp progressed, God was showing me that my perception of Him was warped by my experiences. I not only saw myself in the distorted carnival mirror, but I viewed Him through the same warped mirror.

Not only did I not love Him because I felt He had not loved me, but I didn't trust He was who He said He was! I was a house divided. In my head, I knew that Jesus was my

Savior, and in my heart, I believed God was mean and aloof. My house was built on sand, and it was sinking.

Luke 11:17 reads, "... Every Kingdom divided against itself is headed for destruction, and a house divided against itself falls." This passage is speaking of Jesus driving a mute demon out of a man, when some of the onlookers accuse Him of doing the miracle by the power of Satan. Jesus basically tells them that sort of reasoning makes no sense. Why would the enemy undo the destruction he was trying to accomplish? He was telling them, "You can be assured I am who I say I am." Of course, He didn't use those exact words, but as I read these passages, I knew God was asking me to decide who I believed He was. Was I going to continue to base my perception of His nature on the shortcomings of my mother, the betrayal of my father and the hurts from a fallen world? Or was I going to allow Him to show me what His true nature is?

As I stated before, after my week at camp, I began to read and reread the gospels of the New Testament. What I learned was that Jesus never, ever let the people that surrounded Him down. I didn't read even once where someone said, "Wow, Jesus! You really dropped the ball back there. I'm really disappointed in You." Only when He allowed the world to hang Him on a cross did His friends lose their hope in Him, but only because they did not yet understand what He was actually accomplishing for them and us. Like many of us, they wanted Jesus to do it their way, and they were confused when it didn't happen. I do recall Jesus being let down a few times by other people. But even in those times, when intimately close friends betrayed Him, Jesus was still steadfast in His love for them.

My false perception of the true nature of the Lord was just one more brick in the wall that kept Him locked out of my heart. The truth is the Lord is not a fairy godmother with a wand to bippidy-bop us out of our troubles. He is infinitely more than that. Magic only works in animation, and even then, it only lasts until midnight.

Jesus is holy. He loves His creation, that is, you and me. Sometimes we go through things that are far, far from fair. But I know now that He is big enough to see us through, to use what was meant to destroy us for His glory and purposes.

SURRENDER: WHERE FREEDOM BEGINS

As the kids were trickling into teen camp for the final evening service, my anticipation that there was something better, something more than what I had until now was growing. I was going to hope in the Lord. I could see how He had been with me since I had given my heart to Him and made Him Lord at 21 years old, but I needed to know that He had cared about me before then, also. My anger and disappointment in my circumstances were keeping me from having the relationship with the Lord I desired, and I was ready to lay those feelings down.

Worship started, and everyone joined in with the zeal and abandon that only comes from days spent basking in the Lord's presence. Many had been ministered to in a way only the Holy Spirit can. They were hungry for whatever else the Lord had for them. Like me, many of the young people here this week had experienced a lot of hurt and disappointment in their short lives. It was evident in the dark makeup and clothes, the lack of modesty or, in some cases, the healed cut marks on their arms.

I so badly wanted to protect them from what they might have waiting for them at home. I knew how easy it was to find a little of the peace they were craving in a safe place, like inside of a chapel, then forget the truth they found here when they left this sanctuary.

The desire I had arrived with on Sunday to minister to these young people had only grown as the Lord ministered to my own heart. I wanted to cover them so that what they had received here this week would never be lost or filed away under the heading, "Platitudes I Received Once at Summer Camp." I wanted to cover myself as well. I wanted everything God had for me, wanted to take it home with me. I needed so badly to trust Him. I needed this so I could be different. I wanted to be what He created me to be. I wanted a father, and even more than that, I wanted and needed a daddy!

I had worked so hard, for so long, to control my environment so I could feel safe and secure that I didn't have much wiggle room for normal healthy chaos, like having five children. I wasn't one for highs and lows of emotions or drama of any sort. My house had to be in order and spotless before my head hit the pillow, and I worked out excessively to combat any stress that might have penetrated my defenses.

I wasn't very loving and hated that about myself. I would actually have to make myself say something encouraging or complimentary to my husband or my kids. It was like there was a switch in me that was turned off, or at least set to dim, and I didn't know how to turn it on. It wasn't just God I couldn't show love to, it was everyone in my life I loved.

I desired to give something to these young people around me worshipping, for example, but I knew I didn't have it in me to give. I frantically wanted to be free to love God with all my heart and mind and soul. Fourteen years earlier, I had asked Jesus into my heart to be Lord, not realizing how much I was holding back from Him. I had secretly made a deal with Him: I'll give You what I'm able, and You allow me to keep the pain of my past in the tight grip of control I need it in.

God was showing me that giving up control and allowing Him in was devastatingly painful for a time, but the true freedom His grace brings was the only way to achieve the goal of being everything He created me to be for His glory and purpose.

෧෧෧

I was very fortunate to be involved in the parenting program at the alternative school I attended. The parenting teacher who ran the program wasn't only a teacher to me; she was a friend, advocate and problem solver.

When I told her about my mom leaving, she went to work with me to figure out a solution to my problem. Some of the other teen moms lived in government housing or shared rent with a roommate, so that is where we started. It didn't take long to find another teen mom willing to have me as a roommate. She was a few years older than me, and her son was about the same age as Tiffany.

I moved into her small government-subsidized apartment with her and her son a few days later. My sister chose to live with one of her friends from school. I believe my mom must have given me a number to reach her, but I don't think I contacted her for a while because I was trying to deal with how I felt about her.

It was at that time I began to see my mother for who she really was. This was a devastating blow to my heart. I had already figured out she didn't belong on the pedestal I had placed her on when I was a little girl. Maturity had shown me that. What I was realizing now, however, was that I hadn't been with her when I was little because she hadn't wanted me to be with her. She had probably never wanted to be a mother to me in the way I desired her to be. For all those years, she had left me with this person or that person to go off and take care of herself and her needs and desires. I wanted to scream at her until she felt the pain and despair I felt, but somehow I knew she wouldn't really get it. Any remaining illusions I had of her being the mother I desired were shattered when she left, and that hurt more than anything. The realization that I was truly on my own was terrifying, but I wasn't a quitter. So I started making plans.

The friend I was living with wanted to move into a house with the guy she was dating and offered to let Tiff and I live there with them. The rent was reasonable, and I had no other choice, so we moved to yet another address.

Because I was only 15, I couldn't get a real job. My welfare check barely covered the rent. I felt desperate to be older so I would be capable of improving my situation. I certainly felt older; it just wasn't fair. It made me feel even more trapped to know I couldn't do anything to make things better for us.

My parenting teacher friend got me as much help as she could find. Somebody donated a gift certificate for winter coats from Nordstrom's for both Tiffany and I, along with new shoes for Tiff. I was so thankful for the help she found for us.

I was the youngest teen mother she had had so far, and I think she liked me as much as I liked her. The support I received was great. But it didn't take away the despair over how unfair life could be.

I lived on my own for about a year. It wasn't easy trying to act like a grownup when I just wanted to be a kid. But I did what I had to. I had made some pretty good friends at school. They were there for me when I needed them, as was my parenting teacher. I learned quite a few valuable things from her. For instance, how to make cheese sauce.

You could make anything taste good if you knew how to make a good cheese sauce. She knew some of us teen mothers had to rely on food banks from time to time, and one of the staples at the food bank was mammoth-sized bricks of yellow cheese. With a few dollars worth of groceries and a good cheese sauce, you had a tasty, nourishing dinner. She also taught us that if we didn't like cheese, well, then, we'd better learn to like it because if life hands you cheese, you make cheese sauce!

I always appreciated her pragmatic approach to life. She was never about the drama. I remember being in the nursery one day after I found out my mom was leaving us and having a bit of a breakdown in the nap room. Tiffany was having a tough day, too, and she wouldn't stop crying or lie down for her nap like she was supposed to. After a short power struggle between the two of us, I collapsed to the floor and threw my own fit. My parenting teacher came calmly into the room and picked up Tiff. She then quietly walked out so I could have a cry on the floor in private. She didn't let anyone come in and comfort me or try and get me to stop. She just let me cry until I had calmed myself down and went back to class.

I didn't interpret her actions that day as uncaring. I knew she cared about me. I also understood she knew she could not take me out of my life, and she knew I needed to figure out how to cope in the life I had to live. She was the first strong woman I had known, and I admired her greatly for it.

When I turned 15 and a half, I got my first job. I worked part-time as a hostess at Coco's restaurant. I had become very close to another teen mom at school, and she and her family helped me with Tiff so I could work. I was so excited that I could now do something to improve my situation. I was really only bringing in a few dollars more than my welfare check would have been, but more was more in my book!

I felt incredibly empowered. If nobody else was going to take care of me, so what! I could now take care of myself. Soon I would be 16, and then I would be allowed to wait tables and with that came TIPS! I knew I was going to be fine. I held tighter and tighter to my ability to control the chaos and solve problems on my own. I knew there would be no holes threatening to poke through the dike now!

Not only was I able to achieve a greater sense of control of the chaos around me, but also the chaos inside me. I was only having the occasional anxiety attack now rather than feeling constant fear and dread. I kept busy and focused on what needed to be done from day to day, so I didn't have time for sadness or melancholy.

It didn't take long for my mom's current marriage to come to its inevitable end. She told me I could move back in with her. It was right around Christmas, and she was living in the 300-square-foot shabbily furnished apartment on Highway 99 husband number "whatever" had left her in. So Tiff and I packed up our meager belongings again and moved back in with her.

Although I didn't trust her or see her the way I had, I still felt drawn to the security of not having to watch out for the constant traffic of people who came through the house we currently lived in. Within a couple of weeks, my sister was back with us as well, and we all moved into a bigger apartment. We were all back together again, but I knew I was still on my own. It was clear to me now that I was the only person I could trust to take care of me.

ﾟ◌ﾟ◌ﾟ◌

When I gave my heart to Christ, I didn't realize how much of myself I needed to give to Him. I told Him, "All of me," then held back what I needed in order to feel safe.

As a teenage mom, it was confirmed to me I had to keep things under control if I wanted to feel safe and secure. So I kept for myself everything that was scary and ugly and believed I was better for it. Being out of control was terrifying, so I pretended the things that made me feel weak didn't exist anymore.

The little girl inside me felt like someone I used to know, not someone I used to be. She was a little girl lost, and I believed I was better off not associating with her at all. How many people in the Bible did better when they hid from the Lord? How many stories are there of people being victorious when they snatch control from the Lord and took care of things on their own? Put that way, the answer is pretty obvious, isn't it?

Yet we try so hard to keep things where we can control how they affect us, even if the effect isn't a positive one because the alternative might be too painful. After a while, what we think we are controlling is actually controlling us.

I had a false sense of security that was rooted in many lies. If I keep my house very tidy, it will prove that I am useful, and I will be wanted. If I stay very thin and fit, they will see that I am desirable, and I will be desired. If I don't show weakness, they will know that I am strong enough to be needed. If God never sees what a mess I am and only sees what I have accomplished, then He will know that I am worthy of His love, and He will love me.

I often find my quiet time with the Lord either when I'm lying down to sleep or just waking up in the morning. With all of my kids, this is about the only time I can actually listen to Him without interruption. A couple of mornings ago, while I was contemplating starting my day, I was asking God how to finish this chapter. I was thinking about how scary it is sometimes to totally give everything to Him and trust that He really does want good things for me.

I was reminded of the story of Abraham and his son Isaac. In Genesis 22, God tests Abraham. He says to Abraham, "Take your son, your only son Isaac, whom you love, go to the land of Moriah, and offer him there as a burnt offering on one of the mountains I will tell you about." The Bible tells us it took three days to get there, so for three days Abraham walked with his precious son, knowing what he was going to do at the end of the journey.

I would bet Abraham had many moments along that road where he thought, *Am I really going to do this? Can I really do this?* God brought Abraham to a place of absolute surrender and total obedience. I see Abraham trembling and terrified as he raised that dagger to give everything to the Lord. Those last moments before the angel of the Lord stopped him must have been horrific, but what about those three days?!

Sometimes the road to surrender is the most painful and scary part. But the reward is so worth it! For Abraham it was a promise of blessing on his offspring "numerous as the stars" because of his obedience.

God is asking that we give Him all because He wants to bless us. It isn't about me and what I can accomplish for

Him. It's about Him and what He wants to accomplish in His Kingdom through my surrendered life.

God spoke to my heart through the story of Abraham and Isaac: "If you give Me all of you, it isn't in My nature to hurt you or steal from you, only to bless and prosper you. You can trust Me."

The truth is God wanted to know me, all of me, because I am His child. He wants us to come to Him right where we are. I proceeded precariously through my life on my own strength, believing I was the only path to survival, and it worked … to a point. I had come to camp that week desperately wanting more than moment-to-moment sanity and surviving day to day. What I was coming to realize was that my Father in heaven wanted the same thing for me.

A FIRM FOUNDATION

I showed up for teen camp having made an agreement with God. If this place I was at in my relationship with Him was as deep as I was ever going to get, I was prepared to be okay with it. I was better than I would have ever dared hope. I had more than I ever thought I would in my relationships. I was no longer ever going to be abused physically. I was very well taken care of by my husband in every way. And I had more financially than ever.

But in a way I had given up on giving up. I was trying to figure out how to get rid of the anger that was building and be content without giving my life fully to Him.

On this final evening, I knew my arrangement with the Lord was just another safety mechanism to keep me in the driver's seat and Him in the back. I would allow Him to yell out directions now and again, but I didn't trust giving up the wheel completely. This time, I was going to allow God past my defenses. The freedom I was starting to believe might be available to me was within my reach.

I had spent too long believing my strength was found in my ability to combat all that threatened my wellbeing. I was living with a desperate emptiness I disguised with a matter-of-fact attitude about the abuse I had suffered. God was showing me that the strength I was looking for was found, not in my will, but in my surrender. "I can do all things through Him who strengthens me" (Philippians 4:13).

What that verse doesn't say is how much less energy it takes when you rely on His strength rather than your own. Our strength is in our surrender. I was tired of treading water, always knowing that the river ran deep and was waiting to burst out of its boundaries. I was ready to find rest.

So as we came to the close of camp, I was ready to let go and risk myself like I hadn't in so many years. As I made that decision in my heart, instead of the fear I had expected, I began to feel … relieved.

∾∾∾

After my mom, sister and I were back together, things seemed to get a bit easier. I felt like I had weathered one of those hurricanes in the South you hear about and this was the calm after the storm. There may have been debris scattered about, but all that took was a bit of cleaning. I knew I needed to build my house stronger if I was going to survive the next inevitable storm. Unfortunately, I didn't realize I was still building on sand.

My sister and I got along well, and my mom acted as if nothing had happened to shatter our world. Maybe she was a little remorseful, but I was too disappointed in her to pay attention. This time around we all lived as roommates. We each did our own thing and were each responsible for a portion of the rent. My mom didn't question us about what we were up to, and usually, we were up to a lot.

There were always parties on the weekends, and if those weren't happening, there were underage dance clubs. I always did well in school. I was reliable and mature at work. So on weekends, when Tiffany went to visit her dad, I let loose, pretending to be a free spirit without a care in the world.

I loved that the boys I met while I was out had no idea who I really was or what was waiting for me at home. And I absolutely loved dancing. I would go out on the floor and lose myself in music and movement. I imagined myself living in a gypsy world where I owned nothing and nothing owned me. In my mind it was a world of flowing skirts that made dancing easier, someplace where no worries or responsibilities or predators lived, just music and peace. In reality, it was black lights, big hair and neon colors.

Whether I was in the gypsy world with my eyes closed or neon world with my eyes open, the music was always an escape. It was euphoric to be lost in sound where nothing could touch me. It made me feel powerful, almost like a drug, and since real drugs scared me, dancing was where I would go to turn off the emotions I couldn't deal with.

After I broke it off with Tiffany's dad, I didn't date for a year or so. Eventually, there was a boy; he was cute, and I wanted him to desire me, so I did what came "naturally." I slept with him, even though I had decided I wasn't going to give that away anymore. It was surprisingly easy.

After him there were others. Bit by bit, I gave away

pieces of myself in exchange for affection. I would tell myself it was no big deal. It wasn't "sleeping around" because I only slept with someone if he was my boyfriend, and everybody does that. Unfortunately, just like nearly every teenage relationship, they never lasted forever. I went through a few "boyfriends" over the next several years. I would shamelessly chase after the ones who didn't want me, and get rid of the ones who did. It was becoming increasingly clear to me I was very broken, like some filter or radar in me was malfunctioning, and I didn't have the slightest idea how to fix it.

I was looking for something in those relationships that was always just out of my reach. In the end, I just felt used. More and more I was attracting guys who, at some point, would find me lacking, usually right about the time I was sure I would die without them. I was choosing guys who ultimately would treat me badly. I was never physically abused by a boyfriend. I would have never allowed it to be so blatant. It was usually more subtle. They would cheat on me or just want to be "friends" with side benefits on occasion. Always they would let me know I wasn't quite good enough for them to really love. At every sad ending, I would wish for something better and expect nothing different.

಄಄಄

As I was contemplating writing this chapter, I was going over what it was going to be about and where I found victory in who I am through Christ. It was a tough one for me. I actually let this chapter sit for more than a month as I was going through some tough stuff in my family life. Really, I was using any excuse not to sit down and write about the fact that men other than my husband know what I look like naked. More than anything, I wish that it was only Rick. I realize I was not the only one hurt.

Once things calmed down with our family, I made plans to get back to my writing, still unsure of where I was willing to go with it. All it took was my decision to get back to it, however, for the Holy Spirit to wake me up one morning with a verse. Ephesians 6:12 reads, "For our struggle is not against flesh and blood, but against the rulers, against the authorities, against the powers of this dark world and against the spiritual forces of evil in the heavenly realms." So how does that apply? It is a simple yet very relevant truth: The spiritual world is real and present here on earth.

Because of the choices I made, based on what I had learned from early childhood, the reality was that I attracted and had been attracted to men who treat me badly. I would end up just choosing the best one from that category. I was damaged and used. So I should expect to be treated as such.

Yuck! What a lie! How complete was my state of deception! Sadly I had brought many of those deceitful beliefs about myself into my relationship with God.

"For our struggle is not against flesh and blood ..." If the spiritual world is real, than we are not alone. I don't want to get all freaky on you and have you think you need to be looking under every rock and in every dark corner for what might be lurking there, but the truth is evil exists in the world. And it's really ticked off that it has already lost. The enemy wants to take you down with him.

According to the Bible, the spiritual world is made up of two parts angels to one part demons, right? (Revelation 12:4). So what if someone paid attention to what has been going on in your life since the beginning of it? Let's just say that someone knows where you have been hurt and where you have weaknesses. That someone has watched destructive patterns develop and has encouraged their growth. And even more sinister, that someone is not trying to destroy just you, but also has it in for that abusive guy who just wants to use you for sex. Since you have bought into the lie that you have to give sex for love, whatever twisted love you aren't deserving of, it's the perfect snare for you! This is huge!

Since evil is working at two-thirds less power, they have to be extremely diligent and accurate. They need to confirm in you as quickly and completely as possible that you are worthless. Because ultimately, they aren't just fighting a losing battle, they are fighting a LOST battle!

The enemy isn't going to waste time trying to ruin you with things you don't already have some history with. With me, it was sexual abuse by people who were supposed to love me. He knew I would give sex for love, thereby confirming to myself that I was dirty, worthless used-up goods.

For a boy who is sexually molested by a man, homosexuality is a weapon used against him. Or becoming an abuser himself may be the weapon to perpetuate destruction. A kid who has been physically abused by a parent grows up attracting abusive partners. I could go on and on with examples. I'm not saying these are always the circumstances behind these patterns. But it is a common theme!

So where is the victory? The victory is in the next verse. Ephesians 6:13 reads, "This is why you must take up the full armor of God, so that you may be able to resist in the evil day, and having prepared everything, to take your stand."

The very first thing we need is to accept Jesus as our Lord and Savior. Then, accept every defense He has for you against the arrows of the enemy. Allow the Lord to speak truth into you by reading His Word. Believe He has good things and good intentions toward you, seek His righteousness, relentlessly pray in the Spirit. And finally, put the enemy under your foot where he belongs!

The victory is that I am not defined by what I've done or what has been done to me. I am defined by what Jesus did on the cross. The victory is that I am no longer going to accept what I deserve, but instead I will accept as my lot in life what Jesus says I deserve. *I am a co-heir in the Kingdom* (Romans 8:17).

RECEIVE

This final evening service felt like the crescendo to my week. Every note, high or low, had been leading me to this height. The fear and sadness I had felt at the beginning of the week receded like waves from the beach as the tide slowly goes out. And just as the waves sweep the shores clean, the tears I had shed all week had left me feeling washed rather than drained. Although I probably lost three pounds just in water weight, I felt filled, not emptied!

When my husband and I had spoken to the pastor earlier about what was happening with me and God this week, he had said, "It sounds like you need to know He loves you." Yes, that is exactly what I needed to know. I needed to understand that He hadn't forsaken me all those years ago. There was nowhere to go from here if I didn't get past this place. The question of the week was, "Do You really love me?"

Have you ever been hiking and gotten lost? Heading up somewhere steep enough to see the top but so stuck in the brush you can't figure out how to get there? You try trail after trail, occasionally making your own, but always seem to end up in the same place or worse, a place that is farther away with more difficult terrain. I have been lost like this, and it can get frustratingly scary seeing where you want to be but not seeing how to get there.

First Corinthians 13 speaks of what love truly is. When I read these verses, I could see the love Paul was talking about as a two-way love: from me to the Father and from Him to me. Verse 2 reads, "If I have the gift of prophesy, and understand all mysteries and all knowledge, and if I have all faith, so that I can move mountains, but do not have love, I am nothing." This verse speaks to me of the emptiness I felt playing at this relationship between the Lord and I, knowing I can't really love Him.

This chapter isn't just talking about doing all this great spiritual stuff without love for the Father, but also doing it without accepting and believing in His love for us. That would be religion, and I was tired of religion; I needed relationship.

Deuteronomy 6:5 tells us to "love the Lord our God with all our hearts, with all our souls and with all our strength." He isn't just letting us know He would like us to or suggesting it might be a good idea. This statement is delivered as a commandment, and not just *a* commandment, but the number one commandment!

So if God commands us to love Him, it must mean it's possible. It must be necessary. Above anything else we do in our relationship with the Lord, loving Him is necessary. So I'm asking the Lord on this night, "How?"

ৡৡৡ

When the day finally came for me to graduate from the alternative high school I had attended for four years, I was asked to give a short speech at the graduation ceremony. My grades had always been good, and I had been volunteering to speak at "regular" high schools in their family planning portion of health class. A group of us teen moms would sit on a panel and discuss the realities of having children too young. The idea was, hopefully, to talk kids out of having sex or at least into using contraception. I assumed that was why my school picked me and one other student to deliver the quasi-valedictorian speeches.

On the night of my graduation, I stepped up to the podium and delivered an "I showed you" speech to a small group of parents and relatives, then proceeded to accept my diploma and a small scholarship to community college. I was grateful and pleased with myself for the scholarship, but I had no idea what I wanted to be when I grew up. So I wasn't going to use it. Besides, I knew there were grants and stuff available to me because I was a single mom with no real resources. So I opted to just work for a while until I could figure things out.

I continued working as a waitress because I liked the feeling of having money every night at the end of my shift. Tiff and I moved around the state a bit, half following my mom and her relationships, half following a boy I had met at a concert in Seattle. Eventually, I moved into an apartment of my own.

It wasn't a nice apartment by any means. But Tiff and I were actually on our own and making it! I was just 19, and Tiff was 5. For me, it felt like a huge accomplishment. Our home was in an older complex in Auburn. There was a pool and a decent playground. I furnished the place sparsely with a few pieces of secondhand furniture we covered in sheets and made a large walk-in closet into a bedroom for Tiff.

The boy I was dating at the time was attending the community college in our area, and he impressed upon me that I should be going, too. So I went through the application process and started taking classes for a degree in business. I can't even tell you why I chose business. It probably seemed general enough since I had no real idea of what I wanted to be. The future plans I made had always been based on how to survive the day or week or month, but never really past that.

I tried college, and aside from the English class I loved, I hated it. I disliked the other classes, the teachers and the homework immensely. I just didn't understand the work. Since college made me feel stupid and I was failing some of the classes, anyway, I quit.

It was a stressful time. I tried harder to stay busy so I didn't have time to dwell on a future I knew didn't hold much hope of change for the better. It seemed like I was always trying to "stay busy." I was missing something, needing something, but not knowing what.

I was always trying to stay ahead of my feelings. I would take more hours at work, reorganize my apartment, make goofy plans, whatever it took to try and feel complete, because if I stopped too long, it all felt pointless.

Tiff and I eventually followed the same boy to Alaska where he had grown up. He turned out to be a dead end, but the time in Alaska was interesting. I learned some things about myself while I was there. Most importantly, I learned I don't do well without the sun.

It was dark for 16 to 17 hours every day for the time I was there. I could barely function. I found myself sitting in the dark for hours at a time, just sitting with the lights out, not having the desire to do anything. It was like nothing I had ever experienced. I was depressed, but not in the way I had been in the past. This was more like melancholy, not a fear-based depression driven by anxiety like before, but a sad hopelessness. I didn't have the energy or desire to even get out of bed.

There was a two-week period when Tiff went home to Seattle to visit her dad, and I was left in Alaska by myself, no boyfriend on the scene at that moment. The apartment I rented at the time had a beautiful view of the port in Juneau, with picturesque mountains surrounding it. It was the middle of Alaska's long winter, so everywhere the eye could see was blanketed in the whitest snow. In contrast to the deep darkness of the blue water, it was breathtaking. I knew in my head it was one of the most beautiful places I would ever see in my life. But I couldn't enjoy it because to my heart, it just spoke of loneliness.

As I sat in my apartment with the lights out, staring out the front window, I felt utterly alone: All the beauty was gray. I knew I couldn't stay. The pace was just too slow, and without things to keep me busy and distracted, I wasn't functioning well.

After Tiffany returned from her visit, my mechanism for self-preservation kicked into high gear. I couldn't be left sitting and thinking, so I started making plans to go home. Home?

Alaska was beautiful, but it definitely was not the place for me. Since the boy hadn't work out, either, when the opportunity for Tiff and I to go home became available, we UPS'd our stuff back and jumped on a flight to Seattle.

After the relationship with the Alaskan ended, there were other less serious relationships, all leading me to the same conclusion: There has to be something better than this! And I want it!

As I struggled through those short but tough relationships, I started to feel the pull of anxiety on me again. I needed things to change, and I desperately needed to know that there was some point to why I was trying so hard to survive. I felt as though I was in a race, but I didn't know where or what the finish line was. It was incredibly tiring.

To make myself important, I started collecting things and titles. I got myself through beauty school and got my cosmetologist's license. I wanted to join a gym and found out I could for free if I learned to teach aerobics. I took a course at the gym and became an aerobics instructor.

I convinced my dad to help me buy an overpriced but very cool Jeep and moved into a decent apartment on my own again. I worked hard and paid the bills. I even went to some New Age seminars to see if I could become as enlightened as some of the women in my life I looked up to. The end of the race and the reason for running became less and less clear.

At that time I was very close to a friend from high school. We had been roommates and now lived just a few doors from each other. She had had a child in high school, also, a son, so we helped each other out. We had both been involved in the parenting program, so she had a relationship with my parenting teacher friend, too.

Somehow we had gotten in touch with her again and planned to spend a kid-less weekend at her cabin with her and her husband. My friend was struggling with the same "what's the point?" feeling I was. We shared our feelings with our former parenting teacher, and she gave us some of the best advice I have ever received. She said, "You two need to find a 'run-of-the-mill' Christian church and start attending." I realized she couldn't say that to me as my teacher, but now as my friend she could give whatever advice she wanted.

My friend told me she had grown up going to church with her parents, but after their divorce a few years before, they had all stopped. We both liked the idea and decided we would start looking.

After that weekend, things started moving for me, not in a way I could really describe or necessarily see then, but something was being stirred in me. Now I recognize it as the Holy Spirit getting that Popsicle stick unstuck and back in the current that would continue to pull me toward Him. I wasn't so diligent about finding a church, but the idea sat so comfortably with me, kind of like, "Duh! Why didn't I think of that?" I was overwhelmed with the idea that there had to be something better than what I had experienced so far. A better job, a better boyfriend, a better life! In the midst of this growing desire and intense realization that I SHOULD want something better, I saw Rick.

The story of Rick and I is for another book, I think. But what I can tell you with absolute certainty is that God led me to him and prepared the exact right time for me to really see him and him to see me. I had noticed him often at the gym we both used, but one day, in a moment I won't explain here, I saw him, and I knew he was the beginning of the "something better" I had been looking for.

Rick wasn't in the best place spiritually when we began dating. He had been hurt by a relationship ending abruptly, as well as by people he had trusted in his church. But the thing I saw clearly about him was that he knew his identity. He was a Christian, and no amount of pain, disappointment or rebellion could change that.

Rick likes to think it was his massive arms and devastating good looks that were the things that attracted me so strongly to him. Although those things had me taking a second look, it was Christ in him that drew me in. There was a joy and fullness in him that couldn't be squashed even by the bitterness of heartbreak. He also treated me in a way I had not known before. Even when the times came where we fought or argued, he never demeaned me or said things to wound.

Rick tried on rebellion for a while, just to show God he

didn't care. It was like wearing shoes one size too small: You could squeeze your feet in, but after a while, the fit becomes unbearable. So he told me he wasn't really interested in church, but he took me because he knew Christ was what I needed. I asked Jesus into my heart at the second church Rick and I visited. It was also the second week we were together. I was 21 years old. This time, when I asked Jesus into my heart, I knew I meant it.

Our start was a rocky one at best, with me trying to heal in him what had been broken, and him trying to give me all the love and protection denied me up until then. Really it was just us putting bandages on wounds that needed much deeper healing.

It was at the birth of our first child that Rick understood in an undeniable way God's love for him. Nothing our little girl could ever do would separate her from the love Rick had for her. As I watched the tears roll down his cheeks while he held Kenidy for the first time, a little door in my heart opened just a crack and God said, "This is what a 'daddy' is."

ॐॐॐ

"… But do not have love, I am nothing" (1 Corinthians 13:2). God had led me to this place, this camp, this time with Him. He had shown me an example of His love through my husband's devotion to me and all the blessings in my life. Not just the blessings since finding Rick, but throughout all my life. "Every good and perfect gift is from above ..." (James 1:17). I couldn't deny the truth in those words.

I had received salvation and believed, but He wanted to give me much more. Or maybe, as I was beginning to see, He had given me so much more, and I just wasn't aware of it yet. All of His love and blessings were sitting on the porch of the fortress I had constructed around my heart. The walls had protected me from dealing with the hard stuff, like pain and sorrow, but they had also been the barrier keeping me from receiving good stuff, like the fullness of love and the fullness of joy.

FILLING MY CUP

That last evening of camp, after the message had been heard and the young people had made their way to the front to respond to what would be the last altar call of the week, my trusted friend and I slipped out the side door of the chapel with the pastor to pray in private. As she stood at my side and he stood in front of me, he asked if I was ready to receive God's love.

This time, my answer was, "Yes." He asked me to raise my hands in front of me and turn my hands up, as if I was expecting something to be placed into them. As I did this, he prayed, "Fill her with Your love. Father, fill her with Your love."

It was as simple as that. The terrifying pain and desperate sorrow had slipped away as I had sloshed my way through the last week with the Holy Spirit. All that was left was the pastor saying, "Receive," and me answering, "Yes."

It's hard to put into words how I felt at that moment. It wasn't just an intense moment of feeling, but something that had taken a lifetime to accumulate.

It was momentous, but in a humble way. There weren't any supernatural fireworks or heavenly manifestations breaking into song. I just felt … lighter. It was like a new beginning, a new place to start from. It was the culmination of lots and lots of small victories in the midst of huge tragedies. It was the end of a new beginning, if that makes sense: I was going to build my house on rock, no longer on sand.

The Lord knew I didn't need a big show of His power, I just needed to *know.* When I said yes, I had no doubt He had loved me all along. There was a scene playing in my head of me as a little girl of about 3 or 4 years old. Jesus was holding me above His head, like a father would playfully hold his child, and I was gleefully looking down into His face. Then we were walking side by side, and my small hand was reaching up to hold His much larger hand as we walked. We were outside on soft green grass, and it was a beautiful warm sunny day. I knew in my heart He had loved me then, when I was small, and He loved me now.

I knew He had cried for my pain and been angered to the point of grinding His teeth and balling up His fists when people had hurt me. He had always been my Father. I knew, in that moment, I had nothing to fear from Him. He had been waiting for me to come to Him with childlike faith. Jesus loves the little children.

The pastor gave me an exercise to do every night as I lay down to sleep. He said to ask the Lord to fill me with His love, and as I spoke the words, I was to move my hands in a "scooping" motion, as if I was scooping His love up and pouring it over me. He said I had 30 years of not knowing He loved me to make up for.

That night at camp was "Bon Fire" night. After the service, everyone went back to his or her dorm to change into warm clothes and then headed down to meet at the big fire pit for s'mores and testimonies. There were testimonies of bondages being broken off, relationships restored and truth being revealed. It was awesome to hear the kids give their thanks to Christ for what He had done.

I knew I needed to share my own testimony, if only to establish the truth of it firmly in my heart.

When it was my turn, I started by sharing a bit of my past. I could feel the strength of my female friends and my husband and kids as they rallied around me in support of what God had done. I was able to get through it without crumbling into tears. After a brief background, I shared with them that God had told me He loved me, and this time, I had believed Him. I told them the Lord had been there with me all along, loving me, and I just hadn't seen it.

After I had passed the microphone on to the next person, my two prayer warrior friends pulled me aside and asked to pray with me. They warned me that the enemy would try to steal what had been gained this week. Even as I had barely passed the microphone on, I was beginning to feel shame and embarrassment at what I had just done. I wanted to go hide under a blanket.

I was very grateful for my friends' words. After they had prayed a covering over what God had done, they promised to keep praying for me as I moved into this new place with God.

I walked away from the campfire knowing I had more questions for God. It was like I had gotten a mouthful of delicious truth, and my appetite for more was ravenous.

My pastor friend's parting words of wisdom for me were, "I know you have more questions for Him, more 'whys?' So ask your questions, and He will be faithful to answer." This was the beginning.

EPILOGUE

While I was finishing up the writing of this book, I was visiting my daughter Tiffany, who lives in Texas. My daughter Ryleigh and my son Jaden had accompanied me on that particular trip, and I had sent the three of them to Six Flags for the day. My aged equilibrium doesn't allow me to ride on roller coasters anymore!

Being from Seattle, capital of the latte and home to the original Starbucks, I went in search of a coffeehouse where I could sit and write.

I found a Starbucks (which wasn't easy) and was just getting started when a woman sitting at the table across from me finished praying for the two women she was with. (This is normal in Texas ... and it was Sunday.) The prayer warrior then turned to me and asked if I had any prayer needs.

"Sure," I replied, because at this point I'm always up for what God might want to say to me.

Her word from Him was "comfort." But she kept interrupting herself, saying, "God wants you to know that He loves you." She did it two or three times, then she gave me the verse Jeremiah 29:11. It reads, "'For I know the plans I have for you,' declares the Lord, 'plans to prosper you and not to harm you, plans to give you hope and a future.'" I'll take it!

This verse brought me back to the beginning.

I had believed God was mean and uncaring while I endured the horrible events of my life. But that was not the truth. This verse says it all. "For I know the plans I have for you." He was telling me He knew who I was, and I was significant to Him. My life mattered to Him. "Plans to prosper you and not to harm you." It was never His intention that I be hurt.

Scripture tells me it is the plan of the enemy to kill, steal and destroy. But God's intentions trump the enemy's in the end. "Plans to give you hope and a future." My Heavenly Father wants to give me good things. He wants me to have life and a future full of those good things.

There is no life in lies. Lies steal your future by keeping you walking out your days in circles, repeating the same patterns. There is no future in destination-less circles. You certainly don't see the hero riding off into the sunset with the heroine at the end of the epic battle, only to do a big loop and start the journey again and again. No, of course not. It's a straight road, right into the sunset!

God is good all the time, and that is the truth. He was there loving me and comforting me, even in the darkest hours of my life, waiting patiently for the time when He would draw me up into His lap to hold me and chase away the hurt like only He can.

My Starbucks woman gave me another verse to go with her word about comfort, Psalm 23:4, "Even though I walk through the valley of the shadow of death, I will fear no evil, for You are with me; Your rod and Your staff, they comfort me." This is a very familiar verse, right? It's familiar because it is so relevant to the world we live in. There is hardship, sadness, fear and generally very bad things to walk through, no matter who you are.

If you are alive and you are more than 10 years old, you probably have a concept of "the valley." When I read the words "Your rod and Your staff, they comfort me," I think of power.

My first image is a picture of a very strong man holding a very big stick, a stick able to inflict a lot of damage. What this says to me is: This man is powerful and strong. Even when I am at my weakest, He can comfort me, but in a defensive posture. He will protect me and comfort me while my defenses are down.

Over the years, I had an opportunity to learn what a staff and a rod meant to a shepherd. The rod was a defensive tool to ward off the beasts of the fields, protecting the sheep. The staff was to guide the sheep where the shepherd wanted them to go.

Looking back over my life, Christ was the good shepherd through and through. His staff was there to protect me: I was not torn apart. His rod was there to guide me: It took a while to respond, but His gentle prodding has been there as far back as I can remember.

Matthew 7:24-27 reads, "Therefore, everyone who hears these words of Mine and acts on them will be like a sensible man who built his house on the rock. The rain fell, rivers rose, and the winds blew and pounded that house. Yet it did not collapse, because its foundation was on the rock. But everyone who hears these words of Mine and doesn't act on them will be like a foolish man who built his house on the sand. The rain fell, the rivers rose, the winds blew and pounded the house, and it collapsed. AND ITS COLLAPSE WAS GREAT!"

The verse starts out with "everyone who hears," which is obviously important. But just as important, the scripture continues with "… and acts on them." I did not leave camp perfected, and my life certainly has had some trials. But what I did leave with I have not given back. It is an understanding of my part in the relationship.

A relationship takes two people. God was there for me all along, it was just that I had been building my house on false pretenses of who He was. I can only know Him and be like Him if I spend time with Him. Some of the best times I have with my husband are when it is just him and I without distractions. I know this may seem obvious to some, but it is true with my children as well: The best and most intimate times with them are when we are alone together. This is when I get to know them best. Not what their friends or teachers see, but them — their deepest thoughts, concerns, hopes and desires. It takes time to become intimate in a relationship. With time comes trust, with trust comes love and devotion. I spend time with my Heavenly Father because I want to, not because I have to.

I wrote this book because I want those of you living with a fear of God, as I was, to stop listening to what or who the enemy would have you believe about God. Healing is a process, but I have found it is only possible when Jesus not only becomes your Savior but your Father as well. It is a gift He wants you to have. But He will wait until you choose to receive it from Him. Until you give Him an opportunity to come in and show Himself, He will be waiting.

It's been three years since the Lord birthed in my heart the idea to write this all down. It started as just writing my testimony and morphed into more than that as I prayed for the Holy Spirit to help me get all the words out. There are no words to express how thankful I am for my Father's love. He is more than I knew when I started this project. As I have written the words, He has continued to clear out the lies and shame and replace them with the fullness of His truth and love.

I want you to know that I love and forgive my mom and my dad. I have chosen not to have a relationship with my dad because I felt I needed to protect my kids from the possibility of harm to them. I didn't want to have to explain to them why they had to be cautious of their grandpa. I realized it was possible to love and forgive him and still have boundaries.

My mom is in my life now, and I love her. She has been married to the same man for the last 12 years, and they have built a nice life together. I'm thankful for the husband he has been to her. God has given me a very real peace about my relationship with my mom. I'm happy to have her in my life and thankful she has found happiness in hers.

My sister and I remain very close. She was saved not long after I started going to church. She, like me, was also searching for something good and real, and she has found that in Jesus. She has grown into a beautiful woman of God and devotes her time to raising her very active grandson. I love her and am thankful for her more than I can say.

I was watching an old movie the other day. I had been feeling a bit "under the weather," so I spent all day lying on the couch and watching movies. I was watching the movie *Pretty in Pink*, when right in the middle of it, God reminded my heart of something. There is a point in the movie where the young girl is having it out with her out-of-work, deadbeat dad. He ends up confessing the fact that he hasn't been trying to find a job because he is still too messed up over his wife, who left him three years earlier.

The young girl tells him she misses her absent mother, too, but the two of them have to go on living because nothing will bring her back to them. The dad sees the error of his ways, they hug and he leaves the young girl alone in her pink bedroom. After he leaves, she pulls the picture of her mother off her dresser and into her arms, hugging it to her chest. Then tears silently roll down her cheeks.

I realized I used to be able to do that. I could dredge up memories of my mom or the abuse, and if I dwelled on them for a few minutes, I could bring the despair buried in me to the surface. I would feel the loss all over again. It was what I had constantly worked on so hard for so many years, to stuff down the memories and the feelings that accompanied them.

EPILOGUE

Then it hit me that I can't do that anymore! The despair isn't in me to dig up. It was an incredible feeling to understand the kind of freedom my Father has given me!

Because of the love my Father in heaven has for me, I am able to live a life where my steps lead me forward, looking toward what He has for me, rather than looking back at what already was. Because I finally *chose* to receive that incredible love that had always been there, there has been a restoration in my soul I didn't know was possible!

I want to leave you with just three words ... CHOOSE TO RECEIVE.

ACKNOWLEDGEMENTS

This book would not have been published without the amazing efforts of our Project Manager and Editor, Jane Allen Petrick. Jane's untiring resolve pushed this project forward and turned it into a stunning victory. Thank you for your great fortitude and diligence. Deep thanks to our incredible Editor in Chief, Michelle Cuthrell, for all the amazing work she does. I would also like to thank our invaluable proofreader, Melody Davis, for the focus and energy she has put into perfecting our words.

Lastly, I want to extend our gratitude to the creative and very talented Jenny Randle, who designed the beautiful cover for *The Truth About A Girl: The Story of A Father's Love.*

Daren Lindley
President and CEO
Good Book Publishing

39705365R00104

Made in the USA
San Bernardino, CA
01 October 2016